*Here Am I—Harnessed
to Hope*

Books by Roland B. Gittelsohn

Here Am I—Harnessed to Hope
The Extra Dimension
Love, Sex, and Marriage—A Jewish View
The Modern Meaning of Judaism
Wings of the Morning
Fire in My Bones
The Meaning of Judaism
My Beloved Is Mine
Consecrated Unto Me
Man's Best Hope
Little Lower than the Angels
Modern Jewish Problems

HERE AM I—HARNESSED TO HOPE

Roland B. Gittelsohn

VANTAGE PRESS
New York / Los Angeles / Chicago

FIRST EDITION

Copyright © 1988 by Roland B. Gittelsohn

Published by Vantage Press, Inc.
516 West 34th Street, New York, New York 10001

Manufactured in the United States of America
ISBN: 0-533-07601-3

Library of Congress Catalog Card No.: 87-90205

to beloved friends
who still live
in my mind and heart—

JACOB P. RUDIN
(1903–1982)

THEODORE K. BROIDO
(1927–1984)

*The Lord God called out to the man and said to him, "Where are you? . . . He replied, " . . . I was afraid . . . so I hid."**

—Genesis 3:9 ff.

Some time afterward, God put Abraham to the test. He said to him, "Abraham," and he answered, "Here am I."

—Genesis 22:1

Return to the fortress,
You who are harnessed to hope.

—Zechariah 9:12

*All Bible passages appearing in this publication are reprinted from the *TANAKH*, and are copyrighted (1985) and used through the courtesy of The Jewish Publication Society, Philadelphia.

Contents

*Here Am I—Harnessed
to Hope*

1
Questions

Here am I.

Where? Why? What brought me here? Could I have come any other way? Is my feeling of freedom only a cruel but comforting illusion? Am I really more than flotsam and jetsam, floating aimlessly on the surface of a menacing sea?

How many of the aims I held out for myself half-a-century ago have been achieved? Which were my most serious mistakes? If I had my life to live over, would I do better?

My course has frequently been shifted by the swirls of currents and winds surrounding me, by other people and larger events. Have I, in turn, had any effect on them? Will the world and its human cargo be different—any better, any worse—for my having been here?

These are questions every intelligent person must ask as life advances. If I were the only one to host them in the mysterious hours when sleep teases, there would be no reason to pose them publicly. But I am far from the only one. The man or woman who hasn't been intrigued—at times tortured—by such gnawing uncertainties has stopped living, or perhaps not yet really begun to live.

I had already determined to write such a volume as this, had quietly commenced sorting out recollections and impressions, when a friend reminded me that my own inner compulsion could be reinforced by Jewish tradition. Commenting on the Book of Job, an ancient rabbi re-marked, "Before a person departs this life, God appears

1

to him, saying, 'Make a record of your deeds.' So a person writes, and God seals it."[1]

I would have proceeded even without such authorization, for I remembered a most unusual type of medieval Hebrew literature, the Ethical Will. Generations of Jewish fathers wrote poignant personal testaments bequeathing to their sons and daughters not tangible items of property but traits of character and dedication to a special way of life. I suspected from the beginning—realized more and more consciously as the pages mounted—that this too was among the motives impelling me. In addition to much else, this volume is my Ethical Will.

I have been privileged—in part by choice, in part by chance—to touch upon some of the crucial issues and events of our time. As one who has always placed major emphasis on the counseling aspect of rabbinic work, I have climbed the mountains of exaltation and walked through many valleys of the shadow of death with congregants and friends. I have searched—on their behalf and my own—for answers to the questions that perplex and pain every sentient human being. Why do we suffer so much? Why did my first wife languish for nearly six years in several hospitals before her final release from misery? Is it ever ethical to "pull the plug" when a loved one is ill beyond the possibility of cure? I have confronted this kind of agony, not as an exercise in academic speculation, but in the lurid reality of artificial respirators and intensive care units.

My brain has been picked, my conscience probed by many who sought guidance in their sexual behavior. I have sat long into the opaque hours of night with couples anguishing over the prospect of abortion. With husbands and wives who were either contemplating or regretting adultery. With youngsters who cried for help in handling the nearly intolerable tensions between what they had been taught and the excruciating urgencies of their insistent bodies. With some who were able to disclose their homosexuality only to me. With men or women torn between loyalty to a terminally ill or senile mate and the burgeoning of a new love. Whence have I derived the wisdom and patience needed to help them?

Again and again I have traversed the crossroad where religion and politics intersect. Mine was one of the first pulpit voices in the country to decry our national folly in Vietnam. As a rabbi who cares deeply about the emotional anxieties of his people, how could I preach against American policy in the presence of parents whose sons were fighting in 'Nam, whose son in one instance was already missing in action there? Where did I find support when their understandable resentment was buttressed by a vicious American Legion attack against me? What can a person like myself do when the priorities of priest and prophet clash? How can I justify my insistence on economic democracy to those who provide my income and who perceive my views as a threat to their immediate welfare?

As the first Jewish chaplain in American history to serve in the United States Marine Corps, during combat on Iwo Jima I witnessed human behavior at its glorious best and ugliest worst. How can such saintly and such beastly conduct emanate from one kind of being? How can men hate, not just the enemy, but each other as they bleed and die in what is hailed as their common cause? How can their religious leaders encourage the nastiest of their prejudices? When—as if by a miracle—a man has survived the most terrifying horrors of hell, what can he do to spare his son and grandsons such torment?

As the only rabbi on the Truman Civil Rights Committee, I helped usher in a new era for Black Americans. What do I say or do, how do I act or react when some of the

3

very Blacks I have helped express blatant anti-Semitism?

I am a Zionist—permit me immodestly to say, a leader of American Zionism. No personal achievement is more consistent with my life's theme than serving on the Executive of the World Zionist Organization. I see the State of Israel as indispensable for the survival of my people and its heritage anywhere on earth. I stand taller in the world— as man and as Jew—because of Israel's incredible accomplishments. Yet some trends in Israel distress me immensely. How do I criticize them without handing ammunition to those who aim at Israel's destruction?

I am, or earnestly hope I am, a theologian of the twenty-first century. My religious faith must embrace every truth yielded by science. I cannot, must not ever close my eyes or mind to fact. How can I combine my knowledge with my faith? How cherish the insights of both science and religious tradition in a measure that will preserve and enhance both? How arrive at a framework of faith that will encompass everything I think and do?

Above all, I am a man who sometimes fears the future. The heavy mushroom cloud of nuclear castrastrophe hangs ominously over my head. What can I do to protect my children and grandchildren from imminent disaster?

Have I voiced a fear, posed a problem, expressed a hope you have not known? My quest is yours. My worries and doubts, frustrations and fears, achievements and successes, my incessant search for meaning and faith—all these have also been yours.

Here am I. Here you have been, too. So let us share.

Notes

1. Yalkut Shimoni, on Job. Called to my attention by Rabbi Eugene J. Lipman.

2
Beginnings

None of us is an island. None of us can be understood, can even begin to understand himself or herself, without perceiving the streams of continuity flowing from generation to generation.

I can trace with certainty neither my identity nor my name back beyond my grandparents. There is, to be sure, a family tradition that on my father's side we descend from a renowned sixteenth-century rabbi, Isaiah Horowitz, who wrote his major work—*Two Tablets of the Covenant (Sh'nay Luchot Habrit)*—in Poland and died in Palestine, where he was most probably buried on the Mount of Olives. Of this, I am aware only through dim familial memories. What I know as fact is that my father's father was an eminent Orthodox rabbi, at first in Russo-Lithuania, later in Cleveland. He was born at a time when every male except the oldest son in each family was conscripted into the Czar's army. For Jewish youngsters, this meant virtual servitude for twenty to thirty years. The military training each lad received was more than matched by zealous daily efforts to convert him to Christianity. It became customary, consequently, for each Jewish family to farm out all sons other than the eldest to a family without sons. My grandfather thus became the "only son" of a family named Gittelsohn.

The only known history of the Cleveland Jewish community describes my grandfather as "a quiet, scholarly figure" who was "Cleveland's sole productive rabbinic scholar . . . the scion of a rabbinic line, but his childhood and youth were impoverished. His mother was widowed and the boy was a wandering, hungry *yeshivah* student until his marriage . . . " He is quoted, after his move from Trashkun to Cleveland, as saying, "Here too I found no ease or repose, nor did I have joy or pleasure, (but) thank God who brought me here, I have just a little bit. . . . " Perhaps one reason for Grandfather's lack of pleasure and joy was that, in Professor Gartner's words, "very little local attention was given to his learned accomplishments."[1]

My childhood verbal communication with Grandpa was limited; my language was English, his Yiddish. Our only partial linguistic bridge was Hebrew, which—for him and most Orthodox Jews then—was a tongue for sacred conversation with God, not for ordinary discourse with people. As my sister and I reached the point in our Hebrew studies where we were ready for simple conversation, we would, after careful preparation, address Grandpa in elementary Hebrew phrases. He invariably responded with laughter. At first we were hurt; he was mocking us. Only later did we come to realize that his laughter expressed not ridicule but pride. In a curious way, it was almost as clumsy for him as for us to voice mundane feelings in the sacred tongue.

But emotion often leaps the barriers of language. I remember the smell of Grandpa's beard when he kissed me . . . the stray crumbs in that beard after every meal . . . sitting on his lap while he drank his glass of tea, each sip preceded by biting off half a lump of sugar for himself, gently placing the other half in my mouth. Closing my eyes at this very moment, I still see the combination of regal dignity and paternal love on his face as he conducted the yearly Seder. My heart is tempted to beat wildly again today as I recall standing next to him on the pulpit of his synagogue for my Bar Mitzvah.

Grandfather never learned English. It was enough that he had to adjust to so many strange and threatening new ways. And yet there were evenings—at the end of Shabbat or following a Seder—when the family sat in his living room and someone said something funny in English and from his secluded corner came a hearty laugh. Did he know more than he was willing to admit?

Grandpa was a man of fierce independence; his pink cheeks, blue eyes, red beard, and lilting chuckle all conspired to disguise a stubborn strength. While still in Europe, he kept a Hebrew translation of the New Testament hidden behind other books in his vast library. Few rabbis today are without a copy of the Christian Scripture; for Grandfather then, this was an act of daring defiance. As my father wrote to me three-quarters of a century later, "If any of his enemies—or even friends—had discovered that book in his possession, he would have been kicked out of town in the middle of the night and branded a missionary the rest of his life." Few, if any, of them would have bothered to ascertain his real purpose: his incisive mind insisted that he could not defend Judaism, could not protect it against hostile invasion, unless he knew and understood the source of such invasion.

Benjamin Gittelsohn had little patience for the presumption and pomposity that too often characterize the leaders of religion. Several times he was urged by faithful followers to assume the title of Chief Rabbi in Cleveland. Whatever their motives, his was clear in refusing: he just didn't believe in artificial honorifics and had meager respect for those who did. He was happy to accept the authority earned by his courageous leadership and several brilliant books, but wanted no other.

7

Orthodox rabbis in those days were spared the plague of having to preach once or twice each week. Their role was that of scholar, teacher, and judge, not popular preacher. Grandpa spoke from the pulpit only three or four times a year; when he did—with eloquent vigor—believe me, people really listened!

My father once described Grandpa's preaching in these words:

> My father had the ability to manipulate and mold the minds and emotions of his congregation to such an extent that when he reached his highest peak of ecstasy and enthusiasm, the entire congregation would burst out in tears. You have never seen or witnessed such a sight. . . . Imagine a large group of men, old and young, breathing heavily, sobbing, with tears running down their cheeks into their beards; and the women upstairs crying so loud that one could hear them across the street. That was a sight never to be forgotten, and an art on my father's part that very few preachers could have equalled.

Don't be misled by Father's use of the word *manipulate*. My grandfather's preaching was not the kind of rabble-rousing, hysterical hypnosis through which religious leaders—and politicians—too often take advantage of their listeners' vulnerabilities. His eloquence was aimed at improving their conduct and strengthening their Jewish loyalties. His emotive skill was effective only because it exposed and expressed the highest order of integrity.

Nothing attested more convincingly to this integrity than an experience that took place shortly after his death. Because I was already in my first year of graduate study at the Hebrew Union College in Cincinnati, preparing for ordination as a rabbi, the family agreed that I should have first choice from among Grandfather's books. One Saturday night my father and I spent hours sifting through dust-covered papers and volumes. In a bottom desk drawer, we found a cigar box, not the sleek modern kind, but a large one, six inches or more in depth. It was crammed with uncancelled checks, ranging from fresh, recent ones on top to some already yellowing near the bottom.

A mystery? Not if you really knew Grandpa. He was a persistent fighter for causes, but reluctant to quarrel with people. Whenever he suspected that the person offering him an honorarium—for rendering rabbinic judgment on a matter of ritual, for officiating at a wedding or funeral—had earned his money disreputably or might later return to demand a favor, he would politely accept the check with thanks, then promptly place it uncashed in his private depository. Grandpa must have muddled more checking accounts than anyone else in Ohio.

In my senior year of undergraduate studies at Western Reserve University, it became generally known in the Jewish community of Cleveland that I intended to become a rabbi. A scandalized group of congregants waited upon their venerable leader to ask whether it was true that his grandson was entering what they called "the rabbi factory" in Cincinnati, the major school for educating Reform rabbis. Assured that the rumor was well founded, they indignantly asked what he intended to do about it. His answer— in Yiddish, of course—went approximately like this: "Orthodox Judaism is the only kind possible for you and for me. Knowing, however, my grandson's home background and education, if he were to tell me he planned to become an Orthodox rabbi, I would suspect him of hypocrisy. I want him to become the kind of rabbi he can honestly be."

This was no momentary aberration. A few months before Grandpa's sudden death, my first wife and I in-

9

formed him of our intention to be married the following fall and asked whether he would consent to officiate, together with our own rabbi, in the building of the Reform congregation to which both our families belonged. His answer, characteristically, was, "We'll see," which clearly meant, "If you observe such essential Orthodox marriage rites as covering your heads and reciting the appropriate formulae and including the traditional seven wedding blessings, yes." Unfortunately, Grandpa died before the actual date of our wedding; there was no doubt of his willingness to officiate.

I think of this often in these days when Orthodox Judaism so often means obduracy and obstinance. In my earliest rabbinic years on Long Island, several Orthodox rabbis were among my cherished friends. Of course we didn't agree on matters of religious authority and ritual; that's what made them Orthodox and me Reform. But we respected and liked each other. We could talk together, even on matters of theology. We could work together, and often did. No longer so. Sadly . . . even tragically, no longer so. There is scarcely a single Orthodox rabbi I know in the United States today to whom I can honestly express my religious views without fear of offending and being offended, who will openly accept me as an equal rabbinic colleague.

The pity is that traditional Judaism, which these rigid authoritarians presume to represent exclusively, was seldom so univocal or imperious in the past. Indeed, one of the keys to Jewish survival against all the odds of history has been the flexibility of our heritage, its capacity to change and adapt in the light of evolving circumstance and need.

A strange paradox is to be found here. In some respects Reform and Conservative Judaism can be closer than

Orthodoxy to the essential spirit of tradition. On birth control and abortion, for example. A key passage of the Talmud—repeated verbatim in several places—not only authorizes the use of contraception by a woman but even suggests a specific method. Similarly, pre-modern Jewish law permits abortion in cases where the life or health of a pregnant woman is at stake. Yet today the opposition of many Orthodox rabbis to both birth control and abortion is scarcely distinguishable from that of Catholic authorities. The same is true on autopsy, which Jewish tradition accepts if a human life can thereby be saved but which the leading spokesmen of Orthodox Judaism now reject out of hand.

How can we explain the fact that on issues such as these we who are non-Orthodox rabbis sometimes adhere more closely to the essential values of historic Judaism than do our colleagues who accuse us of negating these values?

Mainly by remembering that fear has much the same effect on groups as on individuals. The man or woman who feels threatened tends to withdraw inwardly, to protect himself or herself by resisting change. So it is with societies. When ghetto walls began to crumble, when Jews were for the first time permitted to study and work and play with non-Jews, when assimilation and intermarriage posed the frightening possibility that Judaism and Jews might disappear from history's stage, the natural resilience of our tradition became congealed, almost fossilized. Reform, Conservative, Reconstructionist, and liberally Orthodox Jews agree that change must continue; they differ only on its extent and the basic premises that must guide it. In recent decades, both here in the United States and in Israel, the voices of my grandfather's liberal Orthodoxy have been muted. The intransigents and extremists have taken over.

I must mention one other respect in which Grandfather was unusual. His early American years coincided with the beginnings of modern Zionism, the movement aimed at the establishment and sustenance of a Jewish State. Strong, at times bitter rejection of Zionism came from opposite ends of the Jewish religious spectrum, from both Reform and Orthodox rabbis. Most Orthodox rabbis opposed the efforts of Theodore Herzl because they believed that in His own good time God would reconstitute the Jewish Commonwealth through the agency of the messiah. To "push the end" by human means was to be guilty of utmost arrogance.

Benjamin Gittelsohn believed in God and yearned for the messiah as fervently as any of his colleagues. Yet he did not thrust the entire responsibility for the future onto God. In good, solid Jewish tradition, he saw human beings as God's partners and human effort as indispensable for the fulfillment of divine promise. He therefore became one of the first Orthodox rabbinic supporters of Zionism. A historian of the Zionist movement writes: "On October 20, 1897 Herzl was told that at a Zionist meeting in Cleveland, where Rabbi Gittelsohn and S. Rocker spoke, many members were signed up."[2]

Grandpa died four months after I had matriculated at the Hebrew Union College, almost as if he had waited, before breathing his last, for another member of the family to continue his rabbinic career. A Cleveland newspaper, in reporting his funeral, added: "Six motorcycle policemen escorted the ninety cars of the funeral procession from the synagogue to the cemetery."[3]

There weren't many Orthodox rabbis like my grandfather two generations ago. There are even fewer now.

Where was Grandma in all this? Aside from the fact that her parents in Europe had shared their modest home with the young couple for several years so that a promising scholar could, without worldly worries, continue his studies, what role did she play? What role could she play, besides bearing and rearing twelve children?

She cooked ... she baked ... she cleaned ... she sewed. My nostrils are still redolent of the aroma of soup and chicken and fish that always greeted us on entering her house. I can't forget the feast she prepared to mark my Bar Mitzvah. There was no caterer or accomodator to help; she did it all. She was a wrinkled, modest, almost meek woman, who basked in the glory of her illustrious husband. She seldom spoke. Whenever Grandpa opened his mouth, however, whether to expound the meaning of Torah or just to say he was hungry, her eyes filled with adoring pride; Moses was speaking again from Sinai!

Notes

1. Lloyd P. Gartner, *History of the Jews of Cleveland* (Cleveland: The Western Reserve Historical Society, 1978) 174, 205.

2. Julius Haber, *The Odyssey of An American Zionist* (Twayne, N.Y., Division of G.K. Hall Co., 1956), 107. Used by permission of Twayne Publishers.

3. *Cleveland Jewish Independent*, 8 January 1932.

3

Closer

Sometimes I lament the fact that I did not have a chance to acquire the proper systematic education you are receiving. Had I had that chance, I would perhaps be a different man now. I would perhaps have followed a different vocation. Not that I would have been more of a success than I am, because to be truly successful one must have those all-important qualities, "push and pull," born into him; and I am rather lacking in them. . . .

I always did admire the person who could get up in front of an audience and, by his or her eloquence, sway the public to a good cause. I have always admired the General with a large army behind him, not for war or conquest or destruction, but for rescue and salvation and reconstruction. Not for oppression and persecution and discrimination, but for love and justice and peace. This is where my inferiority complex comes in: I know my shortcomings. I could never be a leader because I wasn't born to be one. I could never be a shepherd because I wasn't trained to be one. I was born to be a poor sheep, a member of a large flock, a follower, that's all.

Plaintive words like these are a recurrent theme in the letters my father wrote me through the years. They come, not incidentally, from a man who never spoke or even heard a word of English until he was nearly twenty. When my children and my sister's were adolescents, I edited a collection of Dad's letters, from which I shall continue to quote from time to time.

14

Back to my father's diffidence: He was in many respects the most remarkable person I ever knew. What accounts for his self-deprecation? I don't suppose anyone will ever really know. Perhaps his smallness of stature or impoverishment of status as a child; perhaps growing up as the son of a forceful community leader; perhaps the vicious anti-Semitism of his earliest environment; perhaps coming to a country whose mores and language were so strange to him; or perhaps an almost conspiratorial combination of all these and others. Whatever the reason or reasons, and against all the evidence this chapter will adduce, self-esteem was not my father's greatest virtue.

His first years were spent in a small village located in the Russian Pale, the only area where at that time Jews were permitted to live. Home was two tiny rooms inside the synagogue building. The smaller space served by day as Grandpa's "study"; by night, with a straw mattress thrown over a bench, Dad shared it as bedroom with several of his siblings. The larger chamber was kitchen, dining room, and living room for the whole family; on winter nights it also hosted the family goat, source of all their milk.

Education consisted entirely of Hebrew school—ten hours a day, six days a week, forty-eight weeks a year of studying Hebrew, Yiddish, and Aramaic; Bible, Midrash, and Talmud; rabbinic commentaries and codes; probably a smattering also of modern Hebrew literature. No secular education at all. Intellectually and culturally, the world was limited to Judaism and Jews. Russian government authority dictated it that way; the Jews of Trashkun acquiesced.

My father grew to become a sober intellectual, altogether a rational human being. Yet even in his recollections of childhood, there was a seed of superstition that later sprouted into a strain of poetic mysticism. He once stayed awake all night with the synagogue sexton, who

15

didn't dare fall asleep because long before sunrise he had to awaken everyone for morning prayers. For some weird reason—perhaps out of the same morbid fascination that moves my granddaughter now to watch TV horror films late at night—their conversation centered on ghosts.

> . . . they roam around in all the dark streets and alleys. They usually appear in the form of a large black goat with a long beard and long twisted horns, but sometimes they appear as an old woman dressed in black, standing in a dark corner and talking to herself incoherently. . . .
>
> You children, products of a modern, unbelieving world, may not believe these stories. You may even ridicule them. But I am talking about "facts"—things I have seen with my own eyes and heard with my own ears. On a good many dark, cold winter nights, when the wind was blowing fiercely, when the snowflakes were striking against the window-panes above my head, when the doors and shutters and broken-down fences nearby rattled incessantly, when the dogs that accompanied the night watchman at the Catholic Church kept on barking and howling and whining—on such nights as I happened to lay awake on my bed near the wall that separated me from the synagogue, I could hear the dead people come in, one by one; I could hear them open the Ark, I could hear them pray in mournful, crying tones. I could hear their voices rise and fall, synchronous with the howling of the wind and the barking of the dogs; and on one or two occasions I could even discern the voice of somebody who had just died a short time before and whose memory was still fresh in my mind.

As accurately as we have been able to calculate, Dad must have been about eighteen or nineteen years old when he came to this country—young, timid, frightened—able to converse only with his fellow-immigrants and family—a tree rudely torn from its native soil, forcefully transplanted into strange and alien earth. In a year or two of night school, supplemented by two private lessons a week, he learned English and passed off enough academic requirements to qualify for entrance into medical school. The high school examinations were given on the afternoon of Yom Kippur, the holiest day of the Jewish year, a day when observant Jews fast and remain in the synagogue. Just before the appointed hour, Dad managed to leave the service without attracting his father's attention—or who knows, perhaps Grandpa noticed this as he did so many things of which he pretended to be oblivious—go to Cleveland's Central High School for his tests, and return a few hours later to resume his worship.

He often told my sister, Natalie, and me of his dilemma at choosing a profession, the only one of twelve siblings, incidentally, to do so. Painfully torn between medicine and the rabbinate, he often wondered for the rest of his life whether he had made the proper decision. I suspect that if his command of English had been better at that time, he might have followed his father's footsteps. He derived intense joy out of my becoming a rabbi; this would have been obvious even had he not said it many times. On visits to our home—usually for the week of Passover—nothing delighted him more than sitting in the easy chair opposite my desk, discussing aspects of my work, half-reading while really watching me and listening to my telephone conversations. Vicariously, he was living the profession he had almost chosen.

Only once—I must have been fourteen or fifteen years old—Dad asked whether I had ever thought of becoming a physician. My response was immediate and brash: "Definitely not! I don't know what I want to be, but I'll tell you one thing for sure: it's going to be an occupation where my time will be my own, not like your life!" Years later—watching me work far into the night, observing the frequency with which the telephone bell interrupted, seeing

17

me dash off frantically on emergencies—he would smile sweetly and say, "Oh, so your time was going to be your own, eh?"

His days as a medical student were no easier, probably even harder than as a *yeshivah* scholar in Europe. He worked at night in a cigar factory in order to afford the tuition to study by day, stealing a snatch of sleep here and there in class.

Despite his own considerable doubts, he became a remarkable physician, a genuine healer, not just a medical mechanic. He treated whole persons, indeed, entire families. More than once I witnessed his reaching a diagnosis that had been missed by an eminent specialist, successful because he knew the psychological as well as strictly medical circumstances of two or three generations in the same household.

Into his ninety-second year, he was counselor and guide as well as physician to thousands of patients. Our entire family—reaching out even to cousins whom we seldom saw—turned to "Uncle Doc" in every straitened circumstance. He never failed them. Nor any of his patients. A general practitioner, he made house calls at the most ungodly hours, responding from his badly needed sleep to those who hadn't paid their bills, even to those whom he knew to be hypochondriacs. His purpose in life was to help people, not to tell them from some lofty perch that they didn't really need help.

In medicine, as in so many other areas, Dad possessed an insatiable appetite for knowledge; he was never satisfied that he knew enough. Each summer for years he took postgraduate courses at hospitals out of town, usually New York or Boston. From early childhood I remember the wrench of his departures, the loneliness of his absences, the joy of welcoming him back, the little souvenirs and gifts he always brought us. Constantly he kept up with the latest discoveries in medical science. How many times I heard or read of some new theory or cure, mentioned it to him, and learned that he had already explored it and in all likelihood had even tried it in his practice.

Unlike so many physicians, my father was never able to protect himself from the travail of patients by building walls of emotional insulation between himself and them. We could always tell at the dinner table when one of his patients was dying or had died. Nothing excited him so joyfully as delivering a healthy baby; nothing plunged him into such depression and despair as bringing into the world a still-born or defective infant. He often said there was no greater thrill for him than hearing a child's first cry of life. Natalie remembers watching him walk from the garage to our house; she could tell from his stooped posture and ashen countenance when the ecstasy of birth had been twisted into deformity or death.

Incidentally, throughout my adult life, wherever I have lectured or preached, anywhere on this continent, even in Israel, I have met men and women whose parents were married by my grandfather or who, themselves, had been delivered by Dad. At eighty he surrendered his driver's license, promising that he would cease making house calls. We might never have discovered his duplicity had he not been mugged one day while waiting for a bus to return to his office after having visited a patient in his home.

He was in his midseventies the first time he was himself hospitalized as a patient. Much as he had empathized before that with those whom he treated, afterward he said, "Every student in medical school, as part of his training, should be forced to spend at least a week or two as a hospital patient. Only then will he be able to appreciate the needs and fears of those who will come to him for help."

Dad lived for others more than for himself, did much more for others than he ever expected them to do for him. When he was hospitalized four years before his death and I rushed to visit him in Cleveland, his first words to me were: "I don't want to live longer if I can't help anyone." In the nursing home that was his final residence, he was the only man even near his age who insisted on dressing and shaving himself each morning, on walking—however slowly and painfully—to the dining room for lunch and dinner. I joked with him that he carried his walker more than he leaned on it.

Though usually of sober mien, he had a dry, almost impish sense of humor, and revelled in teasing those whom he loved. We were not the only ones who acted as if he were ageless. He himself, nearing the end of his seventies, would unselfconsciously describe a sixty-five-year-old patient as "the old man." Despite his innate shyness, he was a demonstrative man, unafraid to express his emotions. I remember the warmth with which he embraced Mother, the love with which he caressed and kissed his children.

A poignant incident, which took place near the end of Dad's life, reveals much about his attitudes and values. In earlier, more vigorous years, he had said more than once that if he were ever reduced to the condition of absolute helplessness he saw so often in his patients, he "would know what to do about it." The implications were clear.

After he had collapsed and been moved to the nursing home, among my sister's many difficult responsibilities was the dismantling of his office. In consultation with him, she disposed of all the furnishings and equipment, storing his old black medical bag in her home.

One day he asked her to bring him a vial of morphine, which she would find in that bag. Remembering his earlier comments, Natalie was terrified. She called me long-distance for advice. My response, as she now remembers it, went something like this: "Dad, though physically incapacitated, is of thoroughly sound mind. He has a right to make this kind of heavy decision for himself. My recommendation is that you bring him the morphine."

I could well believe Nat when she said later that she didn't sleep a wink that night. With anxious heart and trembling hand, she brought him the morphine, fully expecting him to put it aside and to use it after her departure. Instead, he hobbled with it into his bathroom and proceeded to flush it down the toilet. When her face betrayed undisguised amazement, Dad explained that he had heard on a radio newscast about drug enforcement raids aimed at physicians and their families who were suspected of illegally hoarding narcotics. He feared that she might be in danger if his morphine remained in her possession!

Traces of Father's alternate professional choice never left him. In another atmosphere or climate, he might have become a second Maimonides, successful as both physician and rabbi. His life was an uninterrupted love affair with the Jewish people and their heritage. I wish—now after more than half-a-century as an active rabbi—that I had his profound knowledge of Jewish sources. He never stopped studying Judaism, read voraciously to the very end of his life in English, Yiddish, and Hebrew. This was true even during his active professional years, how much truer after his retirement. Every day commenced exactly the same: breakfast was always followed by his reading six or more chapters from the Hebrew Bible. His self-imposed schedule called for completion of the entire biblical text once each year.

Whenever I came from Boston to Cleveland to visit

him in the nursing home, our opening routine was repeated: immediately after we had embraced and kissed, invariably he would pick up his Hebrew Bible, read me a few verses and say: "You know, Roland, I must have read these words a thousand times, but when I encountered them yesterday a new interpretation came to me." And he would proceed to expand on a novel ethical or philosophic idea. All through the years, his letters were punctuated with appropriate biblical and talmudic references. The arduous study in Europe paid off; his memory and mind were all the dictionary or concordance he needed.

Everything Jewish was precious to him; all Jews were his brothers. During my grammar school years, we lived near a parochial school. As I walked each day from home to school, Catholic boys were embarked on the same mission in reverse direction. It was on these occasions that I was first called "Christ-killer" and "kike." One day I was appalled to witness a group of kids taunting an old Jewish rags peddler, calling him nasty names, throwing stones at him and his horse. I came home in tears. Relating to my father what had happened, I said I couldn't really blame the boys for looking down on the old man; he did indeed look dirty and dishevelled.

Dad listened, audibly sighed, and said, "Roland, that disreputable-looking old man may have been a deeply religious student or scholar in the old country. Uprooted from his surroundings, bereft of status and income, he may be plying his unpleasant trade, suffering daily indignity in order to send his son to college, to help him become a great scientist or musician. It's his tormenters who should be scorned, not he." I have never since seen a peddler or street-cleaner without remembering.

My sister and I were weaned on Zionism. *Palestine* was a sacred word in our household. Dad read or told us stories about the destruction of the Temple in Jerusalem—how the birds carried burning embers in their effort to quench the conflagration, how the priests threw the Temple keys heavenward as they apologized to God for having failed to protect the Holy Place, returning the responsibility to Him. Every birthday and graduation was marked by planting trees or purchasing land for others in Palestine; we could have papered our walls with Jewish National Fund certificates. Long before my mother learned to drive a car, she would spend entire afternoons on the trolley, collecting the modest monies her friends had deposited in their blue and white JNF boxes for the purchase of land and the planting of trees.

At the begining of my very first year as a rabbinical student, Father charged me "to spread the holy gospel of Jewish nationalism." He saw Zionism as the ultimate culmination of our people's history. Speaking of *Tisha B'Av*, the mournful holiday that commemorates the destruction of both ancient Temples in Jerusalem, he wrote:

> . . . that was a terrible day. The Temple, the pride of our people, was destroyed. The little country we called our own—though we very seldom had much to say over it—was demolished
>
> . . . During all the centuries since, our people suffered untold misery. They were killed, burned and crucified. They were persecuted, oppressed and humiliated. They were driven from place to place and made the scapegoat for every kind of misfortune—from earthquake and drought to plague and war.
>
> . . . in spite of all these hardships and handicaps, we are still here, full of life and vigor. Other nations, stronger and mightier, have vanished long ago; their names are almost forgotten. But we are here to tell the tale; we have outlived them all.

. . . Nineteen hundred years of almost continuous suffering have been hard to endure. But centuries ago as we sat on the banks of the rivers of Babylon, we raised our right hands to heaven and solemnly swore: "If I forget thee, O Jerusalem, may my right hand lose its skill; may my tongue cleave to the roof of my mouth if I make not Jerusalem my chief joy."

That was the elixir of life which sustained us in our misery, the powerful tonic which supported us whenever we were about to collapse. We never forgot Jerusalem. We always remembered Palestine. And now, after the long night of exile, we of the present generation have the great privilege of witnessing the beginning of the fulfillment of our sweet dream.

These words were typed seventeen years before the establishment of Israel. Next to the birth of his children, the fifteenth of May 1948 was the most glorious day of my father's life. The founding of independent Israel was for him no less a divinely inspired miracle than the appearance of the messiah would be for a devout Orthodox Jew. His most indelible disappointment was that he was never able to see Israel with his own eyes—he who had so loved it and yearned for it, who had contributed so much to make it possible, he could share its realization only through his reading and his children. After each of my first two visits to Israel, I rushed to Cleveland immediately, replete with diary, projector, and slides. They were never enough for his soul to be sated. My father's heart bled for every Jew who suffered, rejoiced with every Jew who succeeded, beat with extra exuberance for every Jew who reached the shores of Israel.

How did he feel about non-Jews? A simple question, an extremely complicated reply. He always sided with the underdog. The moment his nascent medical practice made it possible, he undertook a journey to Washington. America had barely begun to redeem for him its promise of freedom and opportunity. Already, however, he felt for it so loving a patriotism that he had to visit its capital. Seated on a trolley his first day there, he was asked by the conductor to move; he had innocently seated himself at the rear of the car, where only Blacks were supposed to be. He did move—not to the front, but off the car entirely. He felt so nauseated by his first experience with discrimination against another minority that for the rest of his time in the city he walked to his many destinations rather than even implicitly endorsing prejudice.

His attitude toward Christianity and Christians is much harder to describe. He suspected them, resented them, feared them, admired them, wanted to love them. Often he spoke and wrote about the pogroms in his childhood village, told us how no Jewish child could be allowed outside on Christmas and Easter because the sequel to Christian church services on those holy days was nearly always violence and death to Jews. To the end of his life—after more than seventy years in a kinder Christian environment—he felt chills traversing his spine whenever he walked by a church and saw its cross. No plastic surgery could erase the ugly scars stabbed on a sensitive little boy's heart.

And yet he did describe to us standing outside his town's Catholic church, rapturously devouring the organ music penetrating its thick walls. He was friendly with Christian colleagues and patients, not too many of them, but that was more their choice than his. Every year he drove the whole family past the General Electric Lamp works in East Cleveland to witness and admire the spectacular display of Christmas lights. He was never completely at home in a Christian world, but always tried to judge each individual more by his or her deeds than by the faith he or she professed.

His own deeds more than matched his words. Dad's only problem of self-control was limiting his philanthropies to his means. In good years, whenever he permitted Mother or himself a luxury—a fur coat for her, a new car for him, symphony tickets for the two of them—he increased his contribution to one or more important causes. During the Depression, the thing that bothered him most was the possibility that he might not be able to continue these contributions. Each morning he shined his own shoes in the basement, dutifully depositing in a special box the coins he would otherwise have spent for that purpose, so that at year's end there would be money for philanthropy.

Was Dad a perfect parent? Of course not. Only a perfect person could be a perfect parent; and there has never been a perfect person. Natalie and I resented bitterly the times when a planned picnic or outing had to be aborted at the last minute because of a medical emergency. Many times I wished he had been interested in baseball, as my friends' fathers were. Frequently I accompanied him on his house calls, relishing his company and conversation as we drove from house to house, reading in the car while he attended to a patient.

In an area of parental guidance, where he might have been most expected to succeed, he conspicuously failed. As I reached adolescence, at Mother's insistent urging he gave me several pamphlets on sex to read while waiting for him to complete house calls. Then he would ask whether I had any questions, and that was the sum total of his attempt at sex education.

Mother tried to fill in. One summer we spent several weeks on a farm. She walked me around, using the chickens and cows as audio-visual aids for the introduction of sex. When it came to human beings, she tenderly explained that a seed is planted beneath a woman's heart, a seed that then grows into a baby. So far, so good. But even as a child, I was both inquisitive and brash. When I asked the crucial question, "Who plants the seed?" she responded, "God." In later years I teased her by attributing my interest in sex education—including it in our religious school curriculum and writing several textbooks in the field—to her frailty in passing the buck to God.

Did my father live a happy life? Through placidity and peace, no. Through the achievement of either psychological or financial security, no. Through his children and grandchildren, yes, I think he did; he died before our most painful experiences took place. Above all, through the satisfaction of knowing that he as an individual had substantially served purposes larger than himself, yes, in that respect too, my father was happy. He was not a complainer, and wrote about his inner feelings more comfortably than he could speak of them. So let him express himself—both sides of him:

> Those individuals who have a tendency to show emotion, to complain, to kick, to swear and curse when things go wrong, are just the ones who can bear their adversities easiest. On the other hand, those who never complain, who never kick, who walk around with a set chin and a sphinx-like appearance on their faces, are just the ones who suffer the most. They may lay awake nights—thinking, pondering, worrying.

And to my sister, Natalie, on her seventeenth birthday, comparing life to a diary, each year to another page, he wrote:

> The first part of the book is usually filled with joy, with laughter, with happiness and hopefulness; the second part, with gloom, with despair, with pessimism. Happy is he who

at the end of his journey can turn over one leaf after another, to find that all the pages are clean—no blotches, no ink spots, no dirt marks. Happy is he who can read his book's content without blushing, without feeling remorse. Happy is he who is able to find its pages are filled with beautiful thoughts, with noble deeds and charitable actions.

I haven't said much about my mother or her family, have I? Good reason. I never knew my maternal grandmother; she died before my birth; I was named after her in Hebrew. My mother's father I saw only once. He had been a merchant in the states of Montana and Washington. The family lived a strictly Orthodox home life, keeping kosher under very difficult conditions. I have a feeling their Orthodoxy was more a matter of superstition and habit than of deep religious conviction. But it was consistently observed. In days when ice was the only source of refrigeration, kosher meat was imported about once a month from a hundred or more miles away. Mother was exposed, however, to a predominantly non-Jewish environment. In Missoula, Montana, there were only seven Jewish families. Before coming to Cleveland to visit a cousin—and, most unexpectedly to meet a medical student named Reuben Gittelsohn, fall in love with him, and marry him within a few months—she worked in her father's retail store, selling merchandise and clothing to more Indians than Jews.

Mother often mentioned how lonely and insecure she was as a child. Whatever personal propensity she possessed in this direction was certainly reinforced by demography. There was no Jewish community in Missoula, and Jews were excluded from Gentile camaraderie. So desperate was her need for companionship and acceptance, for finding a place to belong, that at one point—with no perception at all of its theological signficance—she secretly joined the Salvation Army. When her parents discovered what she had done, their punishment must have painfully reinforced her innate sense of loneliness and alienation.

Incredible coincidence! During my early rabbinic years, I attended a dinner party one evening at the home of a congregant. Most of the other guests were strangers to me. For want of any really interesting or important topic of conversation, I asked my dinner partner whence she hailed. She turned out to be the daughter of my grandfather's bitterest business competitor in Missoula, one of the other six Jewish heads of household in town. Her father and my grandfather frequently sneaked out after dark, each to examine the other's store windows. What would the statistical probability be of this woman's and my sitting together at dinner in Merrick, Long Island?

Mother was an emotionally frail person, quite incapable of carrying the full responsibilities of marriage and family. Periodically she would suffer what was mysteriously referred to as a "breakdown," and would go off for a few weeks to live with one of her married brothers in nearby Canton, Ohio. I later learned that the first of these "breakdowns" occurred shortly after her marriage at a very young age.

It could not have been easy for my mother to be wife to a very busy physician. Meals were often delayed; the telephone rang incessantly; the domestic pressures were at times intolerable. Could she have carried her burdens more adequately if married to a different kind of man with a less intense profession? Who knows?

During Mother's "spells" Dad vacillated between tender patience and peevish irritation. Depending upon the season, he would brood silently in the living room easy chair or on the porch swing. I suspect that his problems at home probably made him more sensitive to the emotional ills of his patients, more ready to empathize with their families.

Mother did her best. At times she succeeded, but mostly failed. Yet there were moments I remember with joy. As a little child, my favorite fruit was watermelon. Early one summer, when I had quite forgotten its heavenly taste from the year before, she made me close my eyes and open my mouth, so that she could gently place a bite of watermelon on my tongue and wait for me to squeal with delight. She would, when she could, stand in the kitchen for hours, cooking the gefilte fish I loved, making noodles for the chicken soup I relished, baking the fresh strawberry pie I still insist was the best in the world.

My twenty-first birthday fell at the depth of the Depression, at a time when the bottom had dropped out of our family's economic security. We were not destitute, but every dollar had to be stretched; there were none for luxuries and frills. For dessert at my birthday dinner, Mother turned off the lights and triumphantly carried in the cake she had baked. For weeks she had scrimped wherever she could in order to surround it with twenty-one shining silver dollars.

Her influence on Dad—and, through him, on us—was subtle but important. It was, I believe, largely because of her that my father was the most urbane and Americanized of all his siblings born in Europe. Assuredly, his profession aided in that direction, but Mother augmented and reinforced what might otherwise have remained dormant. She too had been born in Russia; brought to this country, however, at the age of six months, she was more thoroughly Americanized than Dad. She was responsible for her children's being sent to summer camps, as well as for the fact that both of us took piano lessons. Not that her musical efforts on our behalf were entirely successful; my teacher, after two years of trying her desperate best with me—coping with my frequently repeated argument that the piano couldn't really be so important if it isn't normally part of a symphony orchestra—had a "nervous breakdown." While I refuse to count myself totally culpable, I'm sure that my intransigence didn't help the poor woman. I remain to this day a much better debater than musician.

Mother exerted a religious influence on Dad also. He was most probably ready to depart from Orthodoxy on his own. Mother accentuated his religious restlessness, encouraging him to join a Reform congregation and send us children to its religious school. As a consequence, my Jewish education was eclectic: I studied in both a Reform Sunday School and a daily communal Hebrew School; celebrated my Confirmation at our Reform congregation, my Bar Mitzvah in my grandfather's Orthodox synagogue. I feel reasonably at home in any kind of Jewish religious service—Orthodox, Conservative, Reconstructionist, Reform—except the most extreme at both ends of the spectrum. The adjectival label is less important to me than the noun Judaism.

Mother affected me in another way she could scarcely have intended. Very early in life I learned how puzzling, frightening, and often intractable emotional illness can be. More than a few congregants and their families found in me an empathy I might have lacked if my mother had been healthier and my childhood happier.

So there we are. Or, more correctly, here I am. Is there something of Grandpa's cigar box, of Dad's passion for the Jewish people, of Mother's need to be both Jewish and American—is there something of all these in me?

I hope so.

31

4
Myself

I have very few memories of early childhood, almost none. What is even more significant psychologically, most of the recollections I have retained center on humiliation and failure. As a kindergartner, I played the role of Santa Claus in a Christmas play—possibly the only instance ever when a future rabbi portrayed Saint Nicholas! There was no dialogue for me to speak. My total dramatic responsibility was to be pulled across the stage on a sled, ascend from it at the proper time, and carry my sack of gifts into a house. Everything proceeded exactly on cue, with one exception: I was already entering the house before realizing that my precious cargo was still in the sled. The action could not continue until I had frantically dashed back to retrieve it. A perceptive observer might have concluded then and there that years later as an adult I would spend a discouraging amount of time looking for misplaced memos, books, and pens.

Forgetting my speech at a Hebrew School Assembly and failing to retrieve the lost words despite three desperate new beginnings . . . fumbling the ball after one of my infrequent athletic successes in an eighth-grade game of touch football . . . ripping a rear door off my father's brand new automobile by backing it out of the garage carelessly . . . these things I remember! The amusement such recollections bring me now still doesn't totally erase the acute embarrassment they caused me then.

One need not be an expert psychologist to realize that the paucity and selectivity of my childhood memories bespeak a great deal of insecurity. So do many of my remembered dreams in the early years of my professional career. They nearly always focused on frustration and failure. I would be on the pulpit, conducting a religious service, the congregation waiting impatiently, and for the life of me, I could not find the proper page of the prayerbook. A chairman was already introducing me, yet I had forgotten either my notes or the subject on which I was to speak. Attending an important convention, I searched endlessly and unsuccessfully for the room in which my meeting was to take place. Gradually through the years, the incidence of such nightmares decreased, but their earlier recurrence was revealing.

There were also more direct and conscious symptoms of insecurity. I was born prematurely, was abnormally thin, and—though my mother would never admit it—was very homely as a young child. I remained physically clumsy and athletically inferior well beyond adolescence. Gym was always a dreaded school hour; as a high school senior, I was still using an appendectomy that took place shortly before my eleventh birthday as an alibi to escape the gym activities I hated most. Before telephoning a girl for a date, I invariably prepared an outline of proposed conversation, lest there be an embarrassing silence. Though I had a steady succession of girl friends and at least a normal number of dates, each time a girl refused my invitation—however valid her reason—I suffered a severe sense of rejection.

Looking back, it all seems silly. In terms of long-range values, the areas in which I was clearly superior far outweighed those in which I was lacking. My grades were sufficiently excellent to warrant skipping me a whole year in elementary school. Yet that success may well have increased my sense of insecurity, for I was then competing with classmates a year older and physically larger than myself. I was elected to the National Honor Society in high school, to Phi Beta Kappa in my junior year of college, as president of my high school senior class, later as Master Frater of my college fraternity. These last two positions certainly bespoke a higher degree of social sucess than I could then have acknowledged to myself. I was captain of the debating team in both high school and college, winner of a state-wide extemporaneous speaking contest at Cleveland Heights High School, recipient of a Delta Sigma Rho key for forensic excellence at Western Reserve University. And yet. . . .

And yet I felt painfully insecure. Why? Because I was an adolescent, and I suppose it is in the very nature of adolescence to feel insecure. Because my values then were far less mature than my mind. I would have given almost anything to exchange my talents for those of the school's most acclaimed athletic star, who quite probably felt as inadequate in my arena as I did in his.

These traumas of transition from adolescence to adulthood have served me in good stead. Me and many others. In my position as successful rabbi, I inevitably symbolize a large degree of self-confidence and power. My own son was for many years unable to believe that I could possibly have ever suffered the kind of inner fragility he knew. One of my most valuable weapons in counseling young people has been my ability to empathize with them. Openly sharing with them in retrospect my own adolescent turbulence has probably helped more of them than any other technique I might have used.

No subject in the curriculum gave me more intellectual or professional competence than my six years of debating. My high school coach, Clarence P. Drury, was a disciple of Professor Howard Woodward, who coached me in college. Both men stressed the importance of evidence and logic. We were not allowed to write out complete speeches for memorization. The outlines from which we were required to work resembled legal briefs. Each statement or proposition had to follow logically from what preceded it and lead logically toward what followed. We were forced to think on our feet, to scrap what we had prepared, if necessary, in order immediately to counter an opponent's argument.

Other than debating, almost every course to which I was exposed taught me how to absorb facts from a lecture or text, memorize them at least momentarily, then regurgitate them at the proper time on examinations. This, I believe, has been the greatest failure of our American educational enterprise. We have forced students to ingest facts—or alleged facts—without digesting them, without critically analyzing them, without using them as the raw materials for constructing values. Debating taught me to think. To articulate ideas in a rational manner that listeners could follow and recall. To distinguish—though not always with total success—pretense and falsehood from truth.

To some extent, debating also produced a negative effect. It encouraged me to see issues as absolutes, clearly and sharply distinguishable between blacks and whites, right and wrong, true and false. One either won or lost the argument; compromise was a sign of defeat. In later years I had to discipline myself severely to recognize that in most controversies neither extreme view is wholly correct, that an aspect of truth inheres in each.

Another disadvantage emerged from my training in debate. I came to depend too exclusively on reason and logic, too little on emotions. I am still essentially a rationalist; that will become apparent in my later discussion of theol-

35

ogy. I still see emotion without the control of reason as a terrible danger. By the same token, however, reason without emotion can be sterile. Logic is a blunt if not altogether useless instrument in counselling a person suffering psychic turbulence. I have often said in my counselling work that the longest distance in the universe is that which separates the heart from the head. In the human search for God too, reason and fact, while indispensable, are by themselves not enough. To experience human life in its fullest dimension, we must think and feel together.

The work of Drury and Woodward in encouraging me to think was continued later by Abraham N. Franzblau at the Hebrew Union College and William Heard Kilpatrick at Teachers College of Columbia University. The former, then Professor of Jewish Education, was a consummate teacher; we learned more about pedagogy just by watching him than from the content of his discussions. He was almost addicted to the blackboard, constantly held a cigarette in one hand, a piece of chalk in the other. Day after day we waited for him to put the chalk in his mouth while lifting his cigarette to the blackboard. It never happened. What did happen was a constant spur to reasoned inquiry and thought. Abe never assigned readings without first giving us a syllabus of goals to guide our thinking, questions to keep in mind as we read.

Kilpatrick was the only teacher I can remember who, in a lecture hall filled with several hundred students, could conduct the kind of discussion one normally expects when a dozen minds search informally together for answers. More than a few times, after leaving a session with him on the philosophy of education, my mind continued to percolate so effervescently that I rode several stops beyond my subway destination.

Throughout my own teaching career, the most prized compliment any former student could give me was to say, years later, "You know, you often annoyed me by refusing to answer my questions with certainty the way most of my teachers did, but I had to admit that you kept me from mental laziness and made me think my way through to possible answers."

One other aspect of my youthful experience had great bearing on what I later became. I clearly recall going through a period—in late high school or early college—of traumatic tension over the prospect of death. Not in morbid fear that death was at all imminent, but over the whole notion that it would eventually come. Was it a form of egotism, of worrying that the world couldn't get along without me? Or of potential personal frustration, that I might not live long enough to resolve my problems, realize my ambitions? I'm not quite sure.

Two things helped calm my fears. One, that death is common and inevitable for all human beings, no different for me than for anyone else. Two, that the world had existed for billions of years before my birth, with no conscious sense of deprivation on my part, and would continue in the same painless manner for me personally when my life on earth had ceased. I would be missing a great deal, but would not be aware of my loss. With death obviously much closer now in the eighth decade of my life, what bothers me is not the idea that my existence will some day cease so much as the fear lest I live on biologically beyond the capacity for a truly human dimension to my days. More on this fear later.

I worked my way through college—among other ways—by giving private Hebrew lessons. The mother of a youngster whom I taught was dying of cancer. One evening, while the boy's father was driving me home, he wondered out loud whether—in light of the physical pain his wife was suffering and the emotional distress that consequently afflicted him—life was really worthwhile. Many, many times in subsequent years, his aching lament has echoed in memory. I have been most fortunate: despite a full share of personal tension and worry, the years have been good to me. There has nearly always been opportunity for useful, productive work and immense gratification that I could do it. But I have had to sit again and again with altogether decent women and men whose burdens were more than any human being should have to bear. And I have found myself asking, even when they did not, whether for them life was really worth living.

5
Rabbi

It was a totally different world:

Franklin Delano Roosevelt's pressing valiantly to save capitalism from the capitalists . . . Charles Coughlin's obscenely polluting the air waves with his poisonous anti-Semitism . . . Adolf Hitler's insidiously laying the groundwork for his fiendish Final Solution . . . a dress rehearsal for World War II via rebellion by Franco in Spain . . . an independent Jewish State still but the wispiest of impractical dreams . . . Reform Judaism perched timorously between its historic opposition to Zionism and reluctant, philanthrophic acceptance of a Jewish Homeland for other Jews . . . the top annual salary of a newly ordained Reform rabbi—after four years of college, then five years of graduate study—$2,500.

We sweltered in the brutal heat of a Cincinnati sun, starched collars wilting, neckties nearly strangling us, awaiting our cue to commence the processional into the Hebrew Union College Chapel. Finally inside, we moved as if we were automatons, unable or afraid to feel the full impact of emotions. At 2:30 we walked down the aisle as laymen. An hour later we emerged—ordained rabbis.It was 23 May 1936, ten days past my twenty-sixth birthday.

Dr. Julian Morgenstern had held his hands solemnly over our individual heads as he pronounced venerable words of Jewish tradition already inscribed on our diplomas, "*Yoreh, yoreh, yadin, yadin*—he may surely teach, he may certainly judge." These were the operative terms of the rabbi's responsibility through the centuries, the tasks to which my grandfather gave the greater part of his time—teaching and judging. To be sure, he had to study continuously in order to perform these functions properly. But study came in the precious private hours he managed to squeeze into the public time when he taught and judged.

What he taught, clearly, was Judaism—its sources and development, its peculiarity and uniqueness, its essential meaning and relevance to the daily lives of his congregants. What he judged could be the ethical motives and behavior of his people, or such mundane matters as whether this particular utensil or food was kosher. What I was now charged to teach was quite the same, though my modern interpretations would differ on many points from my grandfather's. What I would be called upon to judge—correction: what I would presume to judge, whether called upon or not—would be the ethics of both individuals and societies.

There were no rabbis until after the time of Jesus—priests and prophets, but no rabbis. The province of the priest was to implement the sacerdotal practices of the ancient Temple. The prophet was a moral guide and goad. The priest's purview is easy to understand; the prophet's is far more difficult and complex. I needed to appreciate both, for as a modern rabbi my responsibilities would encompass the boundaries of both.

As priest, I would be expected to officiate at public services of worship, to preside at such ceremonies as weddings, funerals, and Bar Mitzvahs. What would be expected of me, more importantly, what would I expect of myself as a prophet? To answer that, I needed to know the nature of ancient prophecy. The Hebrew prophets were not soothsayers or fortune-tellers. If they presumed to predict the future, and they often did, it was not by tea leaf or crystal ball, but as the meteorologist predicts the weather. He uses his knowledge of nature's physical patterns and laws to forecast the probability of sunshine or rain. Similarly, the prophet used his awareness of nature's spiritual sequences to anticipate what was likely to happen to individuals and nations. My task would be to transpose his message into a more modern key, apply it to issues and problems of which he wasn't even aware.

Can that be done? Is it really possible—without prostituting the intention of Amos or Isaiah—to speculate on what they would say about price-fixing or excessive profits or tax rates? Yes, it is possible. I believed that in 1936; I am even surer of it now, provided one remembers that in the midst even of swiftest change, some things remain the same. The law of gravity, for example. The builder of pyramids and the designer of space ships must reckon with exactly the same law of gravity. For either of them to ignore or defy it, would mean instant disaster. Each, obviously, deals within the context of the knowledge and technology available to him; the basic principles remain the same.

So it is with nature's spiritual norms. Certain kinds of behavior yield predictable consequences, no less today than in the past. True, if Amos or Isaiah were to come alive again today, much would confuse him; he would have to learn a whole new vocabulary. But he would quickly discover that the same moral compass that guided him so many centuries ago could still serve today. He would be convinced now, as he was then, that our universe is governed by moral as well as physical law. He would be certain that neither individuals nor nations can evade the consequences of their deeds.

There was tension between prophet and priest in ancient times. Much of Jewish history can be understood in terms of that tension. The priest sought to serve his people's

41

immediate needs: to comfort them in sorrow, to reinforce their satisfactions and joys, to provide them with the security of ritual, to reassure them in moments of uncertainty and doubt. These were necessary and altogether honorable purposes. But they differed from and were at times inconsistent with the functions of the prophet: to chastise those who had done wrong, to remind them repeatedly by how far they had failed to fulfill themselves morally. Aaron was the priest who helped the people build their Molten Calf. Moses was the prophet who smashed the Ten Commandments into shards when he saw that calf. This was more than mere sibling rivalry; this was the difference between two contradictory notions of leadership.

Small wonder that prophet and priest so often fought bitterly. When their differing and conflicting functions are combined in one individual, there is danger of that person's becoming schizoid. The ancient priest did not have to reprove those whom he tried to help; his job was to comfort the troubled. The prophet did not have to collect a salary from those whom he chastised; his task was to trouble the comfortable. Commencing with the 23rd day of May 1936, I had to attempt doing both. I knew then that it would be difficult. I learned only later how difficult.

Why had I chosen to become a rabbi? Was I still the little boy, trying to please Daddy or to live his alternate choice for him? Was I enraptured by the respect given Grandpa? Was I enticed by the august figure of my own rabbi thundering from the pulpit, secretly hoping to disguise my own inner inadequacies under the camouflaging cloak of his authority?

Sometimes we psychologize too profusely, seeking squalid, unconscious motivations for everything we do. A direct, straightforward reason for doing things becomes suspect. What was my direct, straightforward reason for wanting to be a rabbi? Because I enjoyed and excelled in debating, it was almost a foregone conclusion that my vocation would involve some form of verbal expression, but the rabbinate was not my first choice. I thought I would become an attorney until I discovered that the average member of that profession did not spend most of his time dramatically defending the rights of the disadvantaged—as did Clarence Darrow, one of my early heroes—but sat at his desk for hours busied with dull paperwork.

There was nothing explicitly theological about my decision to be a rabbi. I received no "divine call"; neither, so far as I knew, did any of my classmates. We would have laughed uproariously had any of them made such a claim. In no other faith could this be so, because no other faith is quite like Judaism. We constitute a religion, yes; but not a religion, period. Strands of ethnicity and culture, of peoplehood and nationality, are woven—together with those of religion—into the total fabric of Judaism. To pull out one color or thread would unravel the entire tapestry. More on this in a later chapter.

Similarly, we do not subscribe to hard distinctions between the secular and the sacred. Martin Buber put it very well, "In Judaism, there is only the sacred and the not-yet-sacred." The components of our heritage are as inextricably intertwined as are the fingers of my two hands when I clasp them together. And they can no more be surgically severed than can my fingers be without mutilating them.

Another word about our Jewish concept of the sacred: the Talmud tells us that Rabbi Huna urged his son Rabbah to study with Rabbi Hisda. "Why should I study with him?" the reluctant son asked. "He lectures only on secular matters." When Rabbi Huna asked for evidence, his son responded that he had once attended one of Hisda's classes and observed that the entire time was taken up with a discussion of bodily functions. His father's reaction to this disclosure? "He discusses health matters and you call that secular? All the more reason to study with him!"

Similarly, in the nineteenth century, Rabbi Israel Salanter said, "One should be more concerned with spiritual than with physical matters, but another person's physical welfare is your spiritual concern."

So it is that one can contemplate becoming a rabbi without any conscious theological impulse. In my childhood home, every Jewish festival and holiday was observed with warmth as a human experience, a bond uniting the members of our family with each other and to all Jews. During the week, as often as not, we ate dinner before Dad returned from his house calls. Friday was different. No matter how long the delay, we waited. If necessary, Natalie and I were given a snack to tide us over so that all of us together might welcome the Sabbath with candles, *kiddush*, and song. But in the spirit of solid Jewish tradition, through all our celebration, God was assumed, not explicitly emphasized. It was natural, therefore, that when asked, at my first interview before a faculty committee at the Hebrew Union College, why I wanted to enter the rabbinate, I said I loved the Jewish people and felt this was the most constructive way I could serve them.

Let me not overstate the case. Religion was certainly present, more a seasoning that permeated the entire recipe than an extract concentrated in itself.

During my year as a confirmation student at age fourteen, we were obliged to attend weekly Sabbath services. I enjoyed them greatly, left each week with a glow of inner warmth. So much so that the following year, with no obligation imposed by outside authority, I continued to attend quite regularly and became an usher. Was this part of my love for Jews? Or did it presage a yearning for faith, which became manifest only later? I couldn't have answered then;

44

I'm not sure I know even now.

In any event, whatever my motive or purpose, I entered the Hebrew Union College, studied there for five years, and on that stiflingly hot day in May of 1936 became a rabbi.

Scarcely intitiated into my first pulpit, even before the date of my formal installation, I began to feel the strain that often develops between the rabbinic and lay leaders of a congregation. This is by no means entirely new. As long ago as the ninth century in Babylonia, the struggle between Saadya Gaon, a rabbi, and David ben Zakkai, a wealthy lay leader, was so intense that, though Saadya was eventually vindicated, his health was incurably ruined. In eighteenth-century Surinam, one rabbi was forced to include in his contract that he would always side with the lay leaders of the congregation. The founder of American Reform Judaism, Rabbi Isaac Mayer Wise, was physically assaulted by the president of his Albany, New York, congregation—of all places, on the pulpit, of all times, on one of the High Holy Days!

Knowledge of these precedents and of the sometimes insulting tribulations inflicted upon my grandfather gave me a measure of perspective when this kind of tension became a problem for me. I had been called to serve a new group of fifty-six families in Rockville Centre, Long Island. Very few of them had even belonged to a synagague. Many were not quite sure whether they wanted a rabbi who would lead or one who would cater to all their wants. From time to time, they contested my judgment on matters clearly within my field of expertise. I therefore had to remind them that just as a physician must be presumed to possess more knowledge of medicine than a patient and an attorney more background in law than a client, so I was the expert on Judaism.

In retrospect, I sometimes stretched a valid point too

far. On some matters I was correct: it is for the rabbi, not the congregant, to decide how to define Judaism, on what subjects to preach, whether Jews should have Christmas trees. There are other matters, however, on which a rabbi, while retaining the right to offer advice, should accept the decision by a majority of the congregation's members: the budget, whether or when to construct a new building, whom to employ as principal of the congregational school.

Like many young clergymen, I was in the beginning not yet secure enough within myself always to yield where I should. The facts that I remained in Rockville Centre seventeen years and that our membership grew to more than nine hundred families would attest to a reasonably balanced relationship, though some tension persisted to the very end.

The psychodynamics of such tension are intriguing; they apply to the clergy-laity partnership in Christian churches too. In a very real sense, the male rabbi is a father-substitute to many of his members. The ambivalence they most probably felt toward their biological fathers is transferred to him. With one notable exception: the negative component of the love-hate syndrome felt by child toward parent is more easily and safely expressed against a substitute than against a real father. To paraphrase a statement made many years ago by a psychologist, frequently a congregant tries to choke his or her father, using the rabbi's neck.

This became an especially painful reality to me and my family when we decided to move from Rockville Centre to Boston. After seventeen years, a rabbi who had never served another congregation announced to a congregation never led by another permanent rabbi that he intended to leave. The ensuing imbroglio was shattering! One of our dearest friends—an extremely intelligent woman who had been devoted to us personally as well as to the congregation—waylaid my wife one day after a meeting, offered her a ride home, and proceeded to lambaste her mercilessly. "Anyone else has a right to move from the community . . . You and Roland don't. . . . You belong here. . . . We need you. . . . Anyway, you won't even be happy in Boston." So on and on, until my wife had dissolved in uncontrollable tears by the time I arrived home an hour later. The fact that this woman's father had died when she was a little girl had much to do with her outburst. Daddy was dying again.

Fairness requires that the picture be balanced in two respects. True, a rabbi is vulnerable to hostility that he in no way deserves. But the opposite is equally so: he also receives love far beyond anything he really merits. And he too may be reliving childhood conflicts. In a curiously reciprocal way, at one and the same moment, he is "Daddy" to the congregation while the Board is "Daddy" to him. The very same resentment he may have felt years ago against the restriction on his autonomy imposed by an authoritarian father, he now experiences again vis-à-vis those who would circumscribe his control of the congregation. It helps considerably if both partners to this unique relationship are able to understand their unconscious as well as their conscious motivations.

A fascinating example comes to mind. A president of the congregation had been particularly troublesome to me, nettling me at every opportunity, repeatedly insisting that policy was always to be determined by the Board of Trustees; the rabbi's sole prerogative was to implement decisions thus established. The president's father died. I sat with him that afternoon to express my sympathy and to help plan the funeral. In what was intended as a long paean of praise to his deceased parent, my harasser reiterated endlessly how his father kept tight rein on every detail of their family business even after its control had been technically transferred to him and his brother. He was obviously praising with faint damn. While ostensibly complimenting his father for mental alertness and close attention to detail, he was in fact expressing bitter resentment over being treated as a child. For the first time, his attitude toward me was understandable. The rancor he didn't dare express against an autocratic father had been safely diverted to his rabbi. From that moment on—even while arguing against him—I was unable to feel hostile or angry.

A rabbi's children must often pay a price for his success. In this respect they are like the children of any person in public life. The community expects them to be perfect; other parents demand more of them than from their own sons and daughters. One day when my son was perhaps nine or ten years old, he had an angry wrestling match with a slightly older boy who lived across the street. David came home more outraged than I had ever seen him. After his antagonist's mother had interceded and he had given his version of the fight's origin, she said, "I don't believe you. I should think the rabbi's son would tell the truth!"

My wife and I, after trying to calm David down, said to him, "You go back and tell Mrs. C. two things: first, that the rabbi is satisfied his son does tell the truth; second, that the rabbi's son has exactly the same obligation to speak truthfully that her son has, no more, no less. If Mrs. C. wants to resign from the Temple because of our answer, we can't think of a better reason."

A rabbi and his wife—a minister, teacher, or public official and his wife—may do their best to treat their children normally, to protect them from unreasonable expectations. Others in the community, however, often are less understanding. And the children suffer.

They suffer too—as do the sons and daughters of all busy professionals and executives—from their parents' busyness. As often as not, when David wanted me to take him to a hockey game, when Judy expected me to hear her sing in a choral group, there was a death in the congregation or an important meeting at the Temple which preempted my time. The children resented this, sometimes bitterly. At one point David swore vehemently that after confirmation he would never again set foot in a synagogue. Years later—an attorney with children of his own—he served on the board of a Conservative congregation.

A final footnote on the rabbi's family: his wife, too, is expected by many members to be a paragon of virtue as they choose to define it. Ruth was once severely criticized for wearing open-toe shoes! We were more amused than annoyed, grateful for the fact that no one could ever accuse her of failing to help the congregation, because she went far above and beyond the line of duty. The wives of most young rabbis today—God bless them!—refuse to be enslaved by their husband's profession. They make it clear that the congregation has employed one person, not two, and that they are entitled, if they wish, to follow careers of their own. They, their families, and ultimately even those who complain, are better off in consequence.

There were no women rabbis when I was ordained. There are now more than one hundred, mostly in the Reform and Reconstructionist movements; Conservative Judaism has only begun to ordain women. What special problems will they face, beyond those with which I am so familiar from a male perspective? Only the future will tell. Most of our ordained women have experienced little difficulty obtaining an initial position, nearly if not always as an assistant, in an administrative or educational post. I suspect it may be many years before a large, major congre-

6

Help!

"Rabbi, forgive me for disturbing you. My father's in the intensive-care unit of Newton-Wellesley Hospital ... brought here by ambulance last night ... another massive heart attack. He's being kept alive on machines. The doctor has just told my sister and me he doesn't think there's any chance that Father will regain consciousness or be able to breathe again on his own and has asked whether we want him to 'pull the plug.' We feel torn to pieces, Rabbi ... we can't make that kind of decision alone ... we need your help."

I dropped the work I had been doing, canceled the day's remaining appointments, and within minutes was on my way to the hospital, where I remained with the young man and his sister through the dinner hour and into the evening. How could I refuse? I had confirmed both of them, had only a few months before officiated at their mother's funeral, had married the man and his wife.

There was a time when I would have had no resource other than my own intuition with which to help them. During my student years, the curriculum of the Hebrew Union College contained not a single course in what has since become known as pastoral psychology. It did not take long after ordination to realize what a glaring gap this left in my professional competence. The gap had to be filled. I read avidly, attended many lectures, studied psychiatry at the Karen Horney Institute. All of which has stood me in good stead.

We rabbis sometimes quip that we're the poor person's psychiatrists. True . . . and false. Some men and women do indeed come to us because they can't afford a psychiatrist's fees. Others, because they foolishly suppose that seeking psychiatric help is a sign of weakness rather than the symptom of strength it really is. Still others, because they are afraid or ashamed of being labeled mentally ill. Studies show that more emotionally disturbed Americans turn to their clergy-persons for primary help than to any other profession. Whatever their reasons, congregants do approach us in large numbers for personal therapy, and we must know what to do with them.

We must also know our own limitations. I have at times been horrified to hear colleagues tell of the extremely complicated cases of emotional pathology they undertook to "cure." As well might they, without medical training, try to remove an infected appendix with a rusty knife! Rabbis as well as Christian clergy must know enough psychiatry to know that they are not psychiatrists. They must see themselves as general practitioners, able to distinguish between anxieties they are competent to treat and those requiring referral to a specialist.

There are qualitative as well as quantitative differences between the kinds of therapy that can be provided respectively by psychiatrists and psychologically oriented religious leaders. Neither is entirely right or totally wrong; at their best they complement each other. Psychiatry concentrates on the individual, especially on his or her relationship in early childhood with both parents, and on memories and impressions that were repressed because acknowledging them would have been too painful. Religious counseling, while it can never afford to ignore this dynamic, attempts to provide also a larger framework of meaning for the troubled individual.

As a rabbi, I am convinced that for human beings to attain a comfortable measure of mental health, in addition to releasing childhood repressions and fears into consciousness, draining our psyches of their festering poisons, we must see ourselves as pieces fitting into a jig-saw puzzle. My analogy, of course, is inadequate. We are more than inert matter being manipulated by external forces. Having discerned an overall pattern, we must then, by our own initiative, take deliberate steps to fit ourselves into it.

A chassidic rabbi once prayed: "Lord of the world, how could I venture to ask why everything happens as it does? Why are we driven from one exile to another? Why do our foes torment us so? I do not beg You to reveal to me the secret of Your ways. How could I endure the weighty burden of this awesome knowledge? Ah, it is not why I suffer that I long to know, but only whether I suffer for Your sake."[1]

Even for those who may not believe in God, in sheer psychological and emotional terms this is our most compelling need: to know that the insults and pains we inevitably suffer serve a purpose larger and more lasting than ourselves. For some, a humanistic purpose will suffice. Others yearn for cosmic meaning too. All of us can pay the necessary price in discomfort and distress only if we understand it as the means to an important and enduring end. I shall return to this thought later.

Secular psychiatry risks intensifyng the narcissim that is part of the patient's illness in the first place. We see this at its worst in the flood of self-help books and cults that threaten to inundate us. At every turn we are bombarded by *how to's*: *how to* get rich quickly, *how to* enjoy sex more, *how to* relieve tension and live happily. The religious counselor insists that this obsessive concentration on *me*, far from being the cure, is part of the disease.

Yes, each of us who is emotionally ill must begin by identifying the responsible factors in his or her past. We cannot be cured, however, until we learn to include the Other as a part of Self. I have had psychiatrists and psychologists, thoroughly familiar with all the theories and techniques of their own professions, come to me for help. This is the "plus" I have sometimes been able to give them.

Over a period of years, I led groups of twenty or twenty-five individuals on what Catholics call retreats; my preference was to label them Shabbatons, a term derived from Shabbat, the Hebrew word for Sabbath. We secluded ourselves on each such occasion in a small New Hampshire inn where we could study and search together from Friday to Sunday. The combination of a quiet rural setting, withdrawal from the turmoil and tension of ordinary life, and an opportunity to relate intimately with friends, including one's rabbi, often worked magic. At the conclusion of several such experiences, a participant burst out with a variation of the following: "I don't know why, but I have disclosed things about myself to you fellows that I have never told my psychiatrist!"

As we sat in a circle under the sun at one Shabbaton, summarizing what the weekend had meant, a man in his latter seventies suddenly exclaimed between tears, "I realize for the first time that through the years I have given the least of my energy and time to the things which have meant most to me!" . . . The husband of a woman in public life expressed profusely—probably for the first time in his life—what it meant for him to be the spouse of a woman so much more prominent in the community than himself. . . . An adult son was able to voice resentments against his father that had been repressed since childhood.

Did these weekends produce effective therapy? For

some, I have little doubt they did. Can forty-eight hours cure deep-seated neuroses, untangle the knots in twisted personalities? Most probably, no. But they can offer priceless opportunities to ventilate stuffy psychiatric attics that had never before been opened. Men and women have been able to expose things about themselves that they had previously suppressed, expose them to others who would understand and accept without condemnation. This can be and often is a first step in successsful therapy. Call it preventive therapy if you will—minor, not major, emotional surgery. It illustrates a kind of psychological help that a religious leader may be uniquely able to give.

One of my colleagues suffered a devastating rebuff. A little child in his congregation—walking to the synagogue for a children's holiday service—was struck and killed by a hit-and-run driver. The instant he heard the tragic news, my friend rushed to the child's home to offer consolation and help. The victim's parents turned on him viciously, "This is all your fault! If you hadn't changed the time of services this morning from 10:30 to 11, our son would be alive!" To understand and accept such bitterness, to reach out with compassion rather than resentment after such furious and unjustified attack, required almost superhuman sensitivity and love.

Our clergy role in counseling is neither to preach nor to judge—rather to accept people, even love them, where they are. When we have religious insights of value to a troubled person, these must be offered gently, tentatively, as resources for that person to ponder, to accept or reject at his or her own discretion. This and much more will become clear if we return now to my young friends at the hospital with their excruciating choice between life and death for their father.

How did I help them? First, by patiently listening. By encouraging them to tell me again what had happened and how they felt. When they stopped, I waited, gave them a chance to think, gently asked questions even if I already knew the answers, in order to stimulate further ventilation on their part. I encouraged them to explore the probable consequences of each alternative. Though they had begun by turning to me pathetically, as little children would, almost literally begging me to take them off the hook by giving them the answer, I resisted that temptation, reminding them that they would have to live with their decision, hence they had to feel comfortable with it.

"Does Judaism teach anything that could guide us?" they asked. Yes, our tradition could give them guidance but not an unequivocal decision. It forbids us even to move the pillow of a dying person if, by such movement, the moment of death is hastened. Yet in the next breath it says we need not put salt on such a person's tongue in order to prolong a life that is in any event doomed.

We are told also that if, when a man is dying, the chopping of wood nearby keeps him alert, thereby delaying the instant of death, the chopping may be stopped so that he may die more quickly.

An instructive anecdote: when Rabbi Judah was dying, his disciples gathered to pray for his recovery. Remember: to them, prayer was as efficacious a medicine as our most wondrous miracle drug. At first Rabbi Judah's nurse joined in these prayers. When she noticed, however, the unbearable pain he suffered and realized that he would in any event die soon, she stopped her prayers. The disciples continued. Whereupon the nurse hurled a pitcher out of the house. The noise of its shattering in the street diverted the attention of those who were praying; at that very instant, as their prayers were interrupted, Rabbi Judah died.

In the mid-nineteenth century, Rabbi Hayyim Palaggi, Chief Rabbi of Smyrna, used the story of Rabbi Judah to justify his decision that it was permissible to pray for the death of a woman who was incurably ill, suffering terrible pain. Describing Judah's nurse as "full of wisdom and piety," Palaggi went on to say:

> Therefore we may learn from her this law, that it is permitted to ask mercy for a very sick person that he may die, so that his soul may come to rest. For if this action of hers were not according to the law, the Talmud would not have quoted it. Or if they had quoted it, simply because it was an incident that had occurred, and they did not think that she had done well, the Talmud would have said so. As for the rabbis who continued to pray that he should live, they did not know Rabbi Judah's suffering as much as the nurse did. . . .
>
> As it is said in *The Book of the Pious*, . . . that we must not cry out aloud at the time when the soul is departing, in order not to cause the soul to return and bear more pain. Why did Ecclesiastes say, "There is a time for dying"? It means that, when the time comes for a man's soul to go forth, people should not cry aloud so that his soul should return, for he can live only a short time and in that short time he must bear great pain.

It wasn't necessary for me to translate these allusions into the vocabulary of Newton-Wellesley Hospital. They understood: salt on the tongue means heroic medications; the noise of wood being chopped equals intravenous injections; prayer for a miraculous recovery parallels forced artificial breathing. In saying this much, had I exceeded my own advice not to be unduly directive? I hope not. I think not. My purpose in relating the Jewish heritage to their immediate existential anxiety was to indicate that there is room in Judaism for them to reach either decision without incurring a burden of corrosive guilt.

I asked whether they had additional questions, urged them to think carefully on what we had said, bade them not to reach a decision until after I had left, lest they be even unconsciously influenced one way or the other by my presence. Later they told me how much I had helped them. An hour after my departure, they directed their physician to cease his efforts. The patient died peacefully; I presided at his funeral; brother and sister have been able to live with their decision and their consciences ever since.

Not every quandary of similar nature ends this way. A year or two earlier, I had sat with the wife of a physician who was also being kept clinically alive through technological intervention. The problem was the same. She had been told in no uncertain terms that even if her husband's heartbeat and respiration could be indefinitely sustained, too much brain damage had already taken place for him ever to be more than a vegetable. In this instance—because the medical prognosis was even more conclusive, perhaps also because I was dealing with one who presumably could better appreciate the facts and deal with them—I was more directive than usual. I asked whether she didn't think that, in any meaningful sense, her husband had already died. No response. Pushing further, I spoke of what it would mean to sit for days, for weeks, for months or years beside his inert body, never able to reach him as a person. She replied, with vehemence bordering on anger: "I'd rather have him that way than not at all. I won't be the one actively to end his life. If God wants him, let God take him."

At that point I certainly went beyond the boundaries

of good counseling practice. Instead of understanding and accepting that—for whatever reasons of conscience, of recrimination or guilt—she had made her decision, I continued, "If it had been left to God, your husband would have died several days ago. The fact that his heart still beats, is due to human intervention, not divine preference." My words were wasted. She was adamant. The plug was not pulled. Mercifully, the next day her husband died despite the machines.

I confess to strong resentment and frustration whenever a survivor laments that death came too suddenly. "Would you have wanted him to linger in pain so that you might have had more notice? Would you want her to be paralyzed, to be conscious and aware but unable to communicate so much as a syllable?" More often than I would like to believe, the answer is *yes*. Though I try not to be harsh, not to judge others unless, God forbid, I have been in their place, I can't avoid suspecting that sometimes such men and women are moved by their own neurotic needs, not by altruistic concern and love. There are worse things in human experience than death, many things that are much worse. Sudden, unanticipated, unviolent death can be a welcome friend.

Are we ever justified in taking active steps to terminate a human life? Can euthanasia under any circumstance be condoned? Few questions have troubled me more. For over five years I paid weekly visits to a women's ward in a hospital for chronic disease. I left each time shattered. Not a single one of the twenty-five patients I saw there had the slightest chance of recovery. Most of them no longer recognized even their closest relatives; husbands, siblings, daughters and sons received only blank stares. Those who hadn't withdrawn into catatonic silence spoke only nonsense and gibberish. Or moaned in tones that haunted me night and day.

A bright, articulate attorney in my congregation, while swimming one day in the ocean, was hurled onto the beach by a powerful wave. His neck was broken. Though unimpaired mentally, he was totally quadraplegic, at first incapable of speaking at all, later—with the aid of an ingenious, strawlike tube inserted into his throat—able to gasp out sounds that were scarcely intelligible. On my several visits to him in the hospital, trying to understand him required an excruciating combination of alert listening and mind-reading. There was absolutely no hope for recovery, not even for significant improvement.

As soon as his very bleak prospect for the future became apparent, he was determined not to inflict such prolonged suffering on his wife and children. What he wanted from me was quite clear: would he be sinning if he ordered that the respiratory equipment that sustained his breathing be disconnected? Would that be a violation of Jewish ethics? He had already discussed this with his attorney and his wife. What he needed now from me was, I suppose, a kind of ecclesiastical endorsement.

I explained to him the Jewish view as best I could. I told him about moving a patient's pillow and putting salt on his or her tongue; about Rabbis Judah and Hayyim Palaggi and the *Book of the Pious*. I shared with him the ambiguity and ambivalence of our tradition on so extremely sensitive a decision as this. I refrained from offering him direct advice until he asked, during our third or fourth conversation, whether I understood his feelings. Then, holding his shoulders with both my hands I said, "Yes, Dan, I certainly do. I'm pretty sure that, in your place, I would feel the same way."

In my eulogy for Dan just a few days later, I called him one of the bravest persons I had ever known, adding, "One thing must now be inscribed indelibly on our minds, never to be forgotten. It was not because of weakness that Dan decided as he did, not because he undervalued human life. Quite the contrary! It was because of inordinate, superhuman strength, because he appreciated the true sanctity of human life—when and only when it can be truly human."

Yes, I know: euthanasia is an extremely dangerous weapon; it can be, has been, terribly abused. We fallible human beings ought not usurp the prerogatives of God. I know, I know. But surgery is dangerous too. So are powerful medications. Yet we use them. So must we begin, I am increasingly convinced, the controlled practice of euthanasia. No one person should ever be expected or allowed to make such decisions. Each hospital should have a board—better yet, a series of boards, so that no one individual or group should be called upon to bear such awful responsibility too often. Each board might include a physician, a psychiatrist, a clergy person of the same faith as the patient, a social worker, an attorney. The decision to end a life should be made only by overwhelming majority, perhaps even by unanimous agreement, and always in consultation with the involved family. We have ducked this monumental responsibility too long.

What can a rabbi advise when equally valid ideals seem to be in conflict? This happens frequently; more of our important choices are between varying shades of gray than between black and white.

He had been coming to me off and on for perhaps a year. His wife was seriously ill, had been for a long time. She was a demanding woman. At first her sickness was emotional, but it had become organic now too. Few diseases are exclusively one or the other. They had no children, had been partners in business, lived alone in a small apartment. Now she was bed-ridden, infantile in both attitudes and behavior, destroying him with her need for constant attention. He had not known a single hour of uninterrupted sleep for months. What should he, could he do? How reconcile his sense of obligation to his wife with his own struggle for integrity and survival? It bothered him painfully to think of placing her in a nursing home. It would soon kill him were he to keep her with him.

His dilemma was not uncommon. As the proportion of aged men and women increases, larger numbers of us each year will be faced with it vis-à-vis our parents. Is it better to keep a terminally ill father or mother at home or to place him/her in a nursing home? No stock answer will do for everyone. Many variables are involved. What is the patient's preference? Is a reliable nursing home available in the vicinity? What kind of relationship has existed in the past between the sick person and his/her adult child? Can the necessary medical care be provided at home without risking either the health or family stability of those who will be called upon to give it? These are but a few of the questions that must be asked.

Keeping such a patient at home can be the result either of wholesome or neurotic motives. It can be a manifestation of deep love or of corrosive guilt over past negligence. Wanting to remain at home can be an honest, realistic alternative or an unconscious desire to punish others in the family. Each such case must be judged on its own.

My sister and I faced exactly this problem in the final years of our parents' lives. Mother was strong and vigorous physically but had grown increasingly senile. Dad, mentally almost as sharp to the end as in his prime, had deteriorated physically to the point where he needed help to negotiate even the simplest business of the day. What to do? After agonizing hours of deliberation, we decided that a hospital-type nursing home was the best solution—for them as well as for my sister, the only one who lived in the same city. Kept in her home, neither parent could have received the necessary care and Natalie would have assumed a burden heavy enough to jeopardize her own health.

Our solution was not ideal, but we kept to it without pervasive guilt. We visited as frequently as we could, did everything in our power to make the folks comfortable, demonstrated in every possible way that we loved them dearly. Does our decision influence me when called upon to counsel others in the same situation? Probably. It would be foolish to dismiss the personal experience of any therapist or counselor in advising others. To some extent, I suppose each of us relives his own experience and tries to justify his own course of conduct in guiding others. In any event, I try not to make decisions for counselees. Rather to help them honestly examine their own situation, ask the right questions, and arrive at a response with which they will be able to live comfortably.

Back to my friend whose wife's illness threatened to destroy both of them. My task was making room for him to reach either decision without self-flagellation. Once again Jewish tradition helped. Judaism stresses the value of truth, even tells us that God's name is Truth. Yet there are circumstances in which higher priority is assigned to mercy. One may withhold the truth from a person who is desperately ill if telling it will increase the patient's hazard.

Concern for others is of course an important Jewish ideal. "What is hateful to you, do not do to another." But self-preservation too is valued. Ancient rabbis argued about proper ethical procedure if two men are wandering together in a hostile desert, one of them with a flask of water containing enough to sustain only a single person. If they share the water equally, both will die. The rabbis differ in their decisions, but the most authoritative of them, Rabbi Akiva, rules that he who possesses the flask is justified in using it to save himself: better to rescue one life than to lose both.

Judaism prohibits murder. What if someone carrying a weapon threatens to murder me? If I can save my life by wounding him, I am ordered to do so. If the only way to save myself is by killing him, it is permitted. Self-preservation.

Did the thrust of Jewish tradition help my congregant? He said it did. It helped him think what had at first been unthinkable, then do what he had thought to be impossible. He found a nursing home for his wife, visited her often, and even though she reproached him repeatedly, several years have now passed since her death and he has been able to live guiltlessly with himself.

Guiltlessly. What does that mean? One person can lie awake all night, worried that she didn't serve enough to her guests for dinner; another can feel no remorse after brutally gossiping about a friend. One of the egregious early errors made by many psychiatrists was to assume that their proper function was to erase all guilt from their patients. An unforgivable exaggeration of much religion in the past has been to oppress people with excessive guilt. Today the two extremes are moving toward happy and wholesome compromise.

Guilt is a necessary component of human experience, one of the qualities that distinguish us from all other forms of life. A dog that has chewed its master's slipper is incapable of guilt; it can fear punishment, but is never guilty. A person who has carelessly "chewed" another's reputation can, indeed should, feel guilty. The proper aim of mental therapy is not to eradicate guilt, but to help us experience it realistically in proportion to what we have in fact done. And encourage us to use our guilt toward self-improvement.

Two women may simultaneously feel guilt over the fact that they smoked during pregnancy, yet their guilt can be altogether different. One, who has given birth to a premature infant, feels remorse over the possible harm her smoking may have inflicted on the child. The other harbors similar apprehensions, though her baby was born forty years ago. The first suffers realistic guilt, though prevention would have been healthier than recrimination. The second woman has no right to be punishing herself now; forty years ago no one knew the possible damage of nicotine and tar to a fetus. She did the best she could with the knowledge then available; her guilt may endanger her more than smoking in fact harmed her son.

To sum up on guilt: If I am excessively burdened by guilt over something that in fact I haven't done or that was beyond my power to prevent, if I suffer major guilt over what was in fact only a minor delinquency—I am emotionally ill. If, on the other hand, I am able easily to rationalize my every deed, to convince myself that everything I have ever done is acceptable, to blame all my mistakes on others—on mother, father, siblings, mate, boss, circumstances beyond my control—I am no less ill. A healthy conscience is one of our great glories as human beings, one meaning of being created in the image of God. Too little conscience is as much a symptom of pathology as too much.

My function as counseling rabbi is neither to excuse nor to condemn the behavior of others. Rather to help them judge themselves realistically, to excuse and condemn themselves in proper proportion, to strive for substantial improvement without expecting or pretending perfection.

Like guilt, fear also is an emotion I must help my congregants face realistically. A person incapable of experiencing fear would be constantly exposed to danger, would lack the incentive as well as the adrenalin often necessary to save one's life. But many of us fear needlessly and excessively. Many years ago my family owned a toy fox terrier. When the wind blew, pushing waves against the dock at our summer cottage, Tippie barked furiously. Even on a sunny day, he acted as if the world were about to end. He was frantically afraid of a danger that didn't exist.

Some men and women act similarly. A robber accosted me one night in a public garage, threatening to slash me or beat me up if I didn't hand over my money. Had my heart not pounded furiously in fear, I would have betrayed woeful abnormality. My behavior would be no less abnormal, however, were I to feel such panic because an astrological prediction foretold disaster or because I happened to have been born on Friday the 13th. My fear, like my guilt, must be realistic. This is a truth I first had to learn for myself, then transmit to those who, through the years, have come to me for help.

The pressures bringing them to me have been of two kinds. Sometimes they come from within the individual, on other occasions from external events too traumatic for normal psyches to absorb. One Thanksgiving Eve my wife and I were attending an off-Broadway theatre in Rockville Centre. During the intermission I was paged. Two Long Island trains had collided during the evening rush hour. Many of my members were on those trains. There then began the most harrowing experience of my life, exceeding in horror even the military combat I had known on Iwo

Jima. After all, one expects this kind of shock in combat; the nightmare, moreover, is so widespread that a kind of immunity coupled with disbelief sets in. In a civilian setting, the terror is somehow harder to handle.

During the forty hours commencing at 9:30 that Thanksgiving evening, without surcease or sleep, we drove continually from house to house, sitting for a while with each family whose husband and father had not yet returned home, moving on to the next . . . the next . . . the next. We covered over and over a circle of a dozen residences, almost afraid at each to listen as radio announcers added more names of victims to their previous lists. Seven members of our congregation were killed that night, including a husband and wife together. It was with excruciating pain that I officiated at all their funerals over a single weekend, then counseled their surviving mates and children for many months.

I offered them no easy answers, no theological placebos or bromides. Long before that horrible nightmare, I had learned that the time to prepare people theologically for tragedy is before it occurs. Under the immediate impact of heartbreak or unutterable pain, a firm handshake, a loving hug can be much more eloquent than words. The honest theologican must be willing to say, "I don't know . . . I too cannot fully understand . . . let's search together."

A cherished friend came to me regularly for counseling over a long period of time. He was the closest thing to a modern Job I knew—had lost his first wife to cancer, his post-adolescent daughter to a rare neurological disease, and was seriously ill himself. At one of our meetings, after I admitted that I wouldn't dare try to explain why he had suffered so, he chuckled and told me of a conversation the previous night with a mutual acquaintance. "He asked me what answers you give me. I told him none. He then wanted to know why I continued to see you if you didn't give me answers. I said, 'That's exactly why. Because he's honest with me and doesn't offer me a lot of pap.' "

Not everyone feels that way. One woman never forgave me for trying only to help her discover and depend upon her own resources—the God within her, I said—when her daughter died. A clinical psychologist wrote me an angry letter after her eleventh visit: "I was disappointed because I wanted direction from you . . . and the only advice I left with was to work out deeply personal problems of basic trust and mistrust, and only after that could we discuss questions of theological concepts, of God, etc. . . . I am no longer sure if there is such a thing as a spiritual guide."

Immature people demand immature answers; when necessary, I try to give them. When I confront a person who is potentially mature, however, I refuse to settle for less than his or her best. I must meet each individual not only where he/she is, but also where he/she could and should be.

The difficulties and frustrations I have encountered in my counseling sometimes seemed impenetrable. With proper temperament, talent, and preparation, it's easy to be either a good counselor or a good preacher; it's very difficult to be both. Take the matter of adultery. In public pronouncements, loving Judaism and knowing the ingredients of a good marriage compel me to speak in strongest terms against marital infidelity. In the privacy of my study, the matter is entirely different. The person who, at enormous psychic cost, has just confessed adultery to me doesn't at that moment need a sermon. That person needs to know, from my demeanor as well as my words, that I'm not shocked, that I continue to accept and respect him or her, that I want to help.

This can be, often is, a two-edged sword. The man or woman who has heard me denounce immorality from the pulpit may be extremely reluctant to come to me for counseling, unable to conceive that I may be quite a different person in face-to-face encounter. And I myself have found it very difficult to shift gears, to understand and accept Tuesday afternoon what I have so severely condemned Friday night.

Does this mean that in order to be an effective counselor I must compromise my convictions? Not at all. It means that I must, against the background of unchanged conviction, deal with this person and his or her need at this instant moment. If I am successful in working through the immediate crisis, there may be time later gently to introduce my moral values as the collective wisdom of the centuries, as the sum total of what people in general, Jews in particular, have learned from experience.

It is easier to counsel today than it was fifty-one years ago, because I know more about Judaism as well as the dynamics of human behavior. It is harder to counsel today than it was then because our ethical standards are more complicated with ambiguities. For example: I believe now, as I did then, in pre-marital chastity. Knowledge and experience have conspired to reinforce my conviction that, all else being equal, a man and a woman who have experienced sexual intercourse with no one else have the best chance for happiness in their marriage. But suppose we are dealing with an older couple, a widow and widower perhaps, who love each other and want very much to marry but are prevented from doing so by tax laws that would reduce their combined incomes below the level of decent subsistence. Do exactly the same rules apply there? Or suppose it's a younger couple who will eventually marry but cannot do so now because of parental objection or professional plans. Is their situation the same as that of casual daters?

Yes, I know: a rule once bent can thereafter be more easily broken. But I also know that even if it were possible to apply rules rigidly, it would not always be desirable. Our liberal heritage insists that even the wisest rules are meant to serve people, in the long run to enhance human happiness and growth. This is as true in social ethics as in personal relations. I once stubbornly refused to cross any picket line. My sympathies are still more likely to be with a striking union than with an employing corporation, but I have learned that power can corrupt labor leaders too. My response to pickets can no longer be so automatic.

For years I have opposed, and urged my congregants to oppose, the Pentagon's voracious appetite. Now I want the United States to supply Israel with the arms it so desperately needs. How can I have both? Though I still believe the Defense Department and arms industry to constitute together a major threat to the future of democracy, I must be more circumspect than I once was in opposing inflated budgets for weapons.

Most of my life I have advocated some form of world government, urging that for the sake of peace absolute national sovereignty must give way to international discipline. My ardor in that direction is now considerably cooled by the mischievous UN shenanigans of the Third and Soviet Worlds in prostituting the very meaning of democracy and responsibility. So it goes, both privately and publicly.

Does this mean I am ready to accept situational ethics, the notion that all moral standards are relative and none can be accepted as absolute? Am I ready to agree with a *New Yorker* editorialist that "man . . . draws his principles out of himself: he makes his moral decisions about the value of individual life utterly alone; and those decisions are necessarily relative ones, made in the face of conditions of existence which in themselves have no respect for individual life."?[2]

No, I am not. A degree of truth in the evidence does not justify acceptance of an entire theory. I believe there are binding moral imperatives, eternally valid moral directions embedded in reality. True, they must be implemented—especially when they compete and conflict, one against others—with a generous measure of respect for discrete situations. A norm that should be applied strictly in one instance may well be tempered under totally different conditions. But that does not mean we are doomed to float aimlessly on a sea of circumstance, without overriding guidance or direction.

An analogy will help. If I sail on the lake that is visible at this moment beyond my typewriter, if I sail only for enjoyment, with no purpose other than pleasure, I can let the wind carry me where it will. But there comes a moment when I must return to my cottage. Menacing clouds have appeared . . . dinner time is approaching. Then I can no longer yield to the wind; I must use it for my own purpose, tacking skillfully back and forth, my dock as a primary objective to be reached as speedily as possible. So it is with ethics. In the most urgent crises of life, I must, while allowing for the winds of the moment, know where I want to go. For that, I need direction.

In my hours of counseling, I have touched the lives of people as nowhere else. I sit on the pulpit, during moments of music or silent prayer, looking out at a sea of faces. When I am a guest in someone else's congregation, the faces are anonymous blanks. In my own pulpit, they are known to me, at least many of them are. I am aware of the sorrow or fear in this one's heart, the indecision and doubt in another's, the joyous exultation in yet another's. Sometimes I change a sentence or phrase in my prepared sermon, because my message can be made more cogent for a particular individual who may say to me afterward, "You were talking directly to me, weren't you?" And I wonder silently, "Which others are there here, of whose problems and pains I am unaware? How can I help them?"

Often a rabbi is counseling even when he is least aware of it. At a wedding I spoke to the bride and groom about marriage as the sharing of life's sorrows as well as its joys, about the way in which their love might be deepened by shared sadness. During the reception following the ceremony, a woman we scarcely knew confided to my wife that she and her husband had a retarded child in addition to two normal offspring. "Your husband was so right," she said, "coping with our handicapped son has added a special dimension to the love which has blessed our marriage. We felt as if the rabbi were talking directly to us."

As I look back on my career, I think I may have underestimated the impact of my counseling on the lives of many individuals. At the time of my retirement from active pulpit life, a whole host of people told me—either in writing or to my face—that I had bolstered their spirits at crucial moments of weakness or despair. It has been wonderfully rewarding to know that. Such moments of revelation are not always ponderous. Many years ago a mother in our congregation sent me a poster her four young children had drawn and displayed in their home. Etched in two colors, with an appropriate illustration of a telephone, it read:

IMPORTANT
TELEPHONE
NUMBERS
Fire Dept—332–5595
Doctor—BE 2–2992
Police—527–0030
Poison Center—232–2120
Rabbi Gittelsohn—LO 6–3960

The note attached to this historic document read: "In view of the large size of the Temple Israel congregation, perhaps you may have some concern that the younger members may lose a sense of personal contact with their rabbi. You may find this enclosure reassuring. . . . Since the younger ones may not be quite certain when to call the Poison Center and when to call their spiritual leader, perhaps you had better be forewarned! Thanks for conveying to all your Temple Israel children a sense that you really care."

My counseling has made me more sensitive than I would otherwise have been to others as human beings. It has helped me see the waiter who has forgotten part of my order, the clerk who has treated me brusquely, the driver who has rudely cursed me—to see all of them in my better moments as men and women with heartaches and frustrations similar to my own. Perhaps I just happened to encounter them at a time when the weight was more than they could carry.

Sometimes I don't have to guess. I was caught once in the worst traffic jam I can remember, trapped in a taxi between La Guardia Field and Manhattan, late for an important meeting. My driver, a middle-aged woman, apologized for the delay. After assuring her I realized it wasn't her fault, I said, "It must drive you crazy to do this kind of work." "Oh no," she responded, "this is my relaxation. My agony is at home." She proceeded to gush out her agony: an insensitive, uncaring husband; a twenty-two-year-old daughter married to an abusive man, slowly drinking herself to death. And she herself helpless, unable to do anything. In the midst of congestion that taxed the patience of a saint: "This is my relaxation."

The only help I could give her was to listen sympathetically. I shall never see her again, never know what eventually happened to her. That I have been able to help others more substantially, makes everything troublesome in my life worthwhile.

Notes

1. Buber, *Tales of the Hasidim; The Early Masters* (Schocken Books, 1947), 212 ff. Used by permission of Schocken Books.

2. *New Yorker*, 11 August, 1980. Reprinted by permission; © 1980, The New Yorker Magazine, Inc.

7

Justice

Others have paid a much steeper price than I. Stephen Wise, for example—by any standard one of the most eminent American rabbis of this century.

The scene: Carnegie Hall, New York, where the Free Synagogue held its religious services because it lacked a structure of its own. A public campaign to erect such a building had been announced. The time: a crisp October morning in 1919. The setting: Employees of the United States Steel Corporation were attempting for the first time to organize themselves into a union, rebelling against the arrogant, high-handed feudalism of Judge Elbert Gary, Chairman of the U.S. Steel Board. They were being accused of subversion in every form, of threatening the very foundations of American society. Wise, who had already visited the Pennsylvania mills in aid of the workers' attempt to organize, was about to preach the first of two sermons on the subject.

Just before walking out onto the pulpit, he turned to his wife and said, "Louise, my new synagogue building is going up in smoke today." He had not exaggerated. His sermon topic was "Who Are the Real Bolsheviks?" The thrust of his message was denunciation of the steel executives for denying basic human rights to their workers. Some of his own wealthier Board members, the very individuals on whom he had to depend for Building Fund contributions, owned substantial investments in U.S. Steel. Others feared that the drive toward unionization, if successful in this instance, would soon threaten their industries. So many pledges already made to the Fund were withdrawn as a result of that sermon that the whole program had to be abandoned. It wasn't until five months after Stephen Wise's death three decades later that his congregation was able to dedicate its first synagogue building.

In that memorable sermon of 1919, Rabbi Wise spoke words that I have cherished and tried my best to heed: "I know that there are penalties, many and grave, which are likely to attach themselves to this address. It is clear to me that there are scores of manufacturers, large and small, within the ranks of this congregation, who may for a time in any event take serious exception to my thought. Some of them will doubtless determine to refuse to lend their help to the building of the Synagogue Home that has long been planned. I am ready to bear every burden and to pay every penalty. The one thing I am not ready to do is to conceal my inmost convictions. Better the truth spoken in this hired meeting place, or in the littlest or humblest of meeting places, than concealment of conviction and evasion of truth in the most cathedral-like synagogue structure."

Some Christian clergymen have spoken and acted in the same vein. John Haynes Holmes, a contemporary and close friend of Stephen Wise, was one of them. The Social Gospel movement in early twentieth-century Protestantism was a conscious attempt to direct the attentions of the church toward urgent political and economic issues.

Two pastoral letters issued in this decade by the National Conference of Catholic Bishops—one on nuclear war, the other on economic justice—have excelled in applying the prophetic imperative to contemporary social evils. Yet, when all is said and done, proportionately there has been much more of this social action in Judaism than in Christianity.

This, for three reasons. First, there is in Judaism no concept of Original Sin, no notion that human beings are born either helpless or tainted with evil, from which they can be redeemed only by divine grace or a special act of ritual. Second, our tradition has no doctrine of vicarious atonement. Not even God can atone for my sins. I am told by ancient Jewish teachers that Yom Kippur, the holiest day of the year, can atone only for my sins against God; I can be forgiven for my sins against other human beings only if I ask and receive their forgiveness, then make restitution for any harm I may have caused them. Finally, Judaism teaches its adherents that Creation is unfinished; we are God's partners in completing it. Small wonder that Jews have been so disproportionately active in the struggle against every form of social injustice and oppression.

We are indebted to Professor Yehuda Bergmann for helping us understand that the primary emphasis of the world's major faiths flows from the reactions of their respective founders. Buddha was so embittered by what he saw of society that he became a recluse, withdrawing from social concerns and concentrating almost exclusively on inner contemplation. Jesus was disillusioned by worldly immorality to the point of concluding that not on this earth but only in the Kingdom of Heaven could salvation be achieved. Muhammad was so appalled by human evil that he predicted the destruction of the world; only through faith in Allah and offering their lives to his service could human beings hope for redemption in an afterlife. Moses was the sole exception. Witnessing the agony and pain his people suffered in Egyptian slavery, he jumped actively into the fray, coping with this life and this world, leading the Israelites to freedom.[1]

The ancient Hebrew prophets followed the paradigm of Moses. Take the first Isaiah, for example. He thundered:

> Woe to those who add house to house
> And join field to field,
> Till there is room for none but you
> To dwell in the land!

Innocent, harmless words, aren't they? Until we transpose them into a contemporary key. If the relatively modest concentrations of wealth by landowners in the sixth century before the Common Era aroused Isaiah's ire, can there be much doubt how he would feel about giant agribusiness today? Or about one corporation that controls well over half our nation's automotive production and much of its military manufacturing, which paces pricing for the whole industry, which handles more money in a year than the combined treasuries of forty states? Or about huge corporations that devastate entire cities by unilaterally closing plants without regard for the welfare of communities and employees? Or about General Electric, which, in 1985, spent six billion dollars to buy RCA and made profits of ten billion dollars, yet paid no corporate income tax whatever?[2]

Rabbis like Stephen Wise saw it as part of their responsibility to update the words of Isaiah, to speak in his spirit and name about the fact that the two hundred largest corporations in the United States, which controlled 45 percent of our manufacturing assets at the end of World War II, dominated 60 percent of them in 1980. That 1 percent of our manufacturers control 88 percent of manufacturing assets and reap 90 percent of all manufacturing profits. Isaiah knew nothing of automobiles or steel girders or corporations. But he was thoroughly familiar with greed, with the injustice that inevitably results from too much in the hands of too few.

In like manner, Amos was an expert on the subject of business ethics:

> Listen to this, you who devour the needy, annihilating the poor of the land, saying, "If only the new moon were over, so that we could sell grain; the sabbath, so that we could offer wheat for sale, using an ephah that is too small, and shekel that is too big, tilting a dishonest scale, and selling grain refuse as grain! We will buy the poor for silver, the needy for a pair of sandals.

No trustee of a congregation has ever objected to a rabbi's reading these words from the pulpit or teaching them in a Bible class. It becomes an entirely different matter, however, if he interprets and applies them, if he points out that while they are archaically poetic, their meaning is as relevant and trenchant today as when they were first uttered. Read them again carefully, with mind as well as eyes. Were he alive now, Amos in the very same words would be condemning such specific business practices as using false measures and weights, evading government regulations, charging exorbitant prices, reaping unjustifiably huge profit, selling defective goods, victimizing the impoverished or marginal consumer.

From Moses to Amos to Isaiah to the post-biblical rabbis whose teachings are embodied in the Talmud—a steady, consistent line of pronouncement, with very special emphasis on what we today call business ethics. An example: in Temple times, every Jewish woman was obliged to sacrifice a pair of doves in Jerusalem after each pregnancy, regardless of whether it terminated in a miscarriage or a live birth. These sacrifices were naturally offered on one of the three festivals when Jews would ascend from every part of the land to the Temple. It frequently happened, however, that a woman was unable to make her pilgrimage for several years. In that event, she might well be expected to offer several pairs of doves, not just one. Aware of that, merchants would seasonably increase the price of doves. (Read: law of supply and demand.)

We are told in the Talmud of a time when the price of a pair of doves had been artificially inflated to two golden dinarim, many times their normal cost. Whereupon Rabbi Simeon ben Gamliel decreed that one pair would suffice for each woman, no matter how many times she had been pregnant since giving her last sacrifice. By the end of the same day, doves were selling for one-fiftieth of their price that morning!

Another example: Jews were forbidden from eating any leavened food during the Passover festival. Because earthenware utensils absorb some of the food cooked in them, the rabbis had decreed that such pots must be broken in anticipation of Passover. The sellers of new pots tried to take advantage of this by drastically increasing their prices at the end of the holiday when the old pots had to be replaced. Rabbi Samuel, the chief Jewish legal and moral authority of his day, would not allow such abuse. He immediately threatened that unless the merchants reduced their prices to a reasonable level, he would permit the use of old pots. Prices were lowered at once; ethics had to prevail in the marketplace.

Had there been Chambers of Commerce in those days, the prophets and rabbis would have earned no accolades. Quite to the contrary, they frequently were made to suffer.

Amos was driven back from Israel—where he preached—to his native Judah; Isaiah was condemned as a traitor to the upper class whence he had emanated; Jeremiah was thrown into a prison pit. Nothing quite so drastic has befallen a modern rabbi who takes the prophetic part of his responsibility seriously. Indeed, he is likely to be acclaimed by those of his members who nurture their social consciences. But the more affluent of his constituents, while probably supporting his right to pulpit freedom, will never feel entirely comfortable with his prophetic role. Stephen Wise learned that the hard way.

I have paid a lesser price for trying to instruct the societal as well as the personal ethics of my congregants. Many of my sermons—especially on the High Holy Days, when the largest attendance of worshipers can always be anticipated—have been focused on aspects of business ethics and labor relations and the need for economic democracy. I have been an active member of Reform Judaism's Commission on Social Action since its inception and have fostered a Social Action Committee in our own congregation. On one occasion I organized and led an all-day seminar on economic morality for business leaders in the congregation.

Few of my efforts in this direction have aroused so much antagonism as my revisions of liturgy. One of the most impressive of our traditional prayers for the Holy Days is a litany entitled *Al Chayt—For the Sin*. Each line is introduced by the same formula; each then continues with a specific kind of malfeasance for which we ask forgiveness. My congregants never seem to be more than mildly uncomfortable about acknowledging such sins as those caused by *abuse of power* or *disrespect for parents and teachers* or *hardening our hearts*. These, after all, are categories vague and general enough not to be threatening.

Oh what a difference, however, when I asked them to confess: "For the sin we have committed by *false advertising . . . by manufacturing and selling inferior goods . . . by put-*

ting property and profit ahead of human welfare." Seldom did the Day of Atonement pass without several angry letters. Year after year the matter was discussed by the Ritual Committee and Board of Trustees. Finally, by way of wholesale response, I preached a sermon—on Yom Kippur, of course—entitled *When Prayer Pinches.* In it, I cited specific examples of the economic sins castigated in my innovative liturgy: a U.S. Senate estimate that deceptive packaging and promotion in the food industry alone cost American taxpayers 14 billion dollars a year . . . a *Wall Street Journal* report that the annual loss to American consumers due to short-weighting and counting ranged between 1.5 billion and 10 billion dollars . . . documented evidence of toys that can easily cripple or kill the children who play with them, of new school busses with such potentially fatal defects as faulty brakes, flimsy clutches, and leaky gas tanks. I quoted passages from the Talmud that prohibited specific categories of business immorality still profusely practiced today.

And I concluded, "Some of you have accused me of being stubborn on this point. You are correct. I *am* stubborn and intend to continue so. When I stop being thus stubborn, you had better reexamine my qualifications to be your rabbi."

Sermons can be effective, but only as starters. This is the difference between a sermon and a lecture: the purpose of the latter is to convey information; of the former, to motivate changes of attitude and behavior. I am always more than mildly annoyed when, after I have preached my heart out, a congregant says, "I enjoyed your sermon." The aim of preaching is not to provide enjoyment. It would be a far better compliment to say, "Your sermon made me feel uncomfortable," or, "I'm going to have to do something about that."

82

Because I expect my sermons to produce action on the part of listeners, I have always felt they must be associated with action also by me. When I invite contributions to a cause, I must myself contribute as generously as I can. When I preach on behalf of business ethics, I am obliged to put the strength of my arms where my mind and mouth are.

I have therefore worked actively on behalf of such organizations as the United Farm Workers. It has been my good fortune to know Cesar Chavez personally, to meet with him several times and appear with him on television. He is, in my judgment, one of the most deeply, devoutly religious men I have ever known. Supporting him has meant—at times when growers were ruthlessly oppressing the workers in their fields—approaching congregants who own a large supermarket chain to urge that they join in boycotting non-union lettuce and grapes. To their credit, be it said that on at least some occasions they cooperated to their immediate economic disadvantage.

For the same reason and in the same vein, more than once I have joined delegations of religious and labor leaders to visit the executives of retail department stores, asking them to refrain from selling products manufactured by the J.P. Stevens Co., a firm that through the years was notoriously calloused to the rights of its workers and that reached a settlement with them only in 1980. It would be foolish to pretend that such efforts always succeed, or that they meet with the approval of most business people in the congregation. But we have achieved our purpose at least partially more often than I might have expected.

I guess in the last analysis the difference between my views and those of our economic overlords boils down to this: they strive to behave as ethically as possible while achieving a desired level of profit; I believe they are entitled to as much profit as they can obtain while acting ethically.

For me, this is a matter of more than just good economics or effective democracy. It is also a dictate of my religious faith, a directive from Judaism, which orders me, in God's name, to guard the rights of the powerless against the privileges of the powerful. "Justice, justice you must pursue!"

Business is only one of the areas where I have tried to apply the ethics of my heritage. . . .

. . . My first thought was that a prankster was calling, a friend, no doubt, successfully disguising his voice. "Rabbi Gittelsohn? This is the White House calling. The President plans to appoint a special Civil Rights Committee and wants to know whether you would be willing, if chosen, to serve. You understand, this isn't official and must be kept confidential; we're just inquiring about your availability."

It was no hoax. The voice, I learned later, was that of David K. Niles, President Truman's advisor on minority groups.

There were fifteen of us on the Truman Civil Rights Committee, including leaders of the three major religious groups, of business and labor, of the political, academic, and black communities. For nearly a year we met twice a month in Washington, each time for two days. The President himself joined us for our first and final sessions. Our report, published near the end of 1947 and entitled *To Secure These Rights*, presaged virtually all the advances made on the civil rights front since.

Proposals that we now take for granted—perhaps too much so—were revolutionary then: a permanent national Commission on Civil Rights . . . restrictions on police brutality and related crimes . . . anti-lynching legislation . . . elimination of poll taxes . . . granting of citizenship without regard to race, color, or national origin . . . removal of discrimination and segregation from the armed forces . . . protection of public workers against excessive and unreasonable loyalty checks . . . conditioning all federal grants-in-aid on the absence of discrimination . . . enactment of fair practice acts by both federal and state governments in the fields of employment, education, and housing . . . laws prohibiting discrimination in interstate transportation and providing equal access to all places of public accommodation. And so on and on.

In how many of these areas have the goals of our committee been fully achieved? None. In how many has substantial progress been made? Nearly all. The dauntless mettle of a president who was willing to challenge the inlaid bigotry of his own state laid the groundwork for a civil rights movement that went far toward changing the face of our nation. For many on the Truman Committee, our work was the result of political and social forces. For Bishop Henry Knox Sherrill, Bishop Francis J. Haas, and myself, it was also in the deepest sense possible an expression of religious faith.

I remember our first meeting in the White House. We wanted to initiate our efforts with a dramatic, bold demonstration of what we were all about. What better way than by challenging the prejudice of Washington itself? So we telephoned the Mayflower Hotel, one of the city's most prestigious establishments, and made a luncheon reservation in the name of the President's Committee. An hour later we deployed ourselves strategically to enter the hotel's main dining room, where, so far as we knew, no Black had ever been seated. Six whites led the procession; seven of us brought up the rear; securely ensconced in the middle were our two black members, Sadie Alexander and Dr. Channing Tobias. A table large enough for fifteen had been set in the very middle of the room. Too late for any skillful maneuvering that would put Channing and Sadie unobtrusively in a corner! A sacred icon had been shattered.

Today no one even turns a curious head when Blacks are seated in hotel dining rooms. That's progress. But how many Blacks can afford the privilege? In 1978 the gap between family income of Blacks and Whites in the United States was only two percentage points less than it had been in 1945. Between 1972 and 1975, the proportion of black families earning more than $24,000 a year declined from 12 percent to 9 percent.[3] In 1979 the unemployment rate among black adult males was 2.3 times higher than among Whites, the largest margin ever recorded. Black teenage unemployment, which had been 16.5 percent in 1954, had by 1979 risen to 36 percent.[4]

As a result of my inclusion as the only practicing Jew on the Truman committee, after our report had been issued, several Jewish communities invited me to speak. One of them was Birmingham, Alabama. A high-school classmate who lived there asked me in advance to join him, his wife, and a group of their friends for drinks and snacks at their club after my lecture. This, forgive me, was to be a feather in their cap—kidnapping the guest speaker for their little group. My address was bold and direct. After summarizing the report in general terms, I spoke of our specific and special responsibility as Jews to reinforce the rights of other minorities, especially of Blacks.

I have been received more enthusiastically elsewhere. My hosts were obviously embarrassed. We sneaked into the club as inconspicuously as possible, consumed our drinks with indecent dispatch, and departed with all deliberate speed. The atmosphere throughout the community was hostile enough so that, for the only time I can recall outside of military combat, I literally feared for my life. It was with an audible sigh of relief that I left town the following morning. Almost forty years have passed and the atmosphere throughout the South has changed considerably, but I have never since been invited back to Birmingham.

Another Jewish group that asked me to speak on the Truman Report was in Savannah, Georgia. The meeting there was held in the synagogue itself. During the question-and-answer period following my address, I was asked from the floor whether I knew that two black youngsters had approached the president of the congregation before the meeting started, inquiring if they could attend. After much flurry and fluster, he had told them they could stay to hear me, provided they sat in the balcony. Did I know that?

I did not. I was furious. With no attempt to be tactful, I responded that of all places, in a synagogue—of all subjects, at a lecture on civil rights—such behavior was inexcusable. Had I known what had happened, I concluded, I would have gone to the balcony with the two Negroes and given my address there to them.

I had completely forgotten the entire incident when, many years later, I was privileged to meet Dr. Walter J. Leonard, then Assistant to the President of Harvard, later himself President of Fisk University. He described the whole sequence of events that night in Savannah, including a verbatim account of my reaction to the questioner. In response to my puzzlement, he explained, "You see, I was one of those two black youngsters. Rather than sitting in a segregated balcony, my friend and I went outside, stood the entire time by an open window, and heard every word of your lecture. I'll never forget it!"

Amos lived at a time, twenty-eight centuries ago, when his nation was largely led by chauvinists who ascribed every virtue to themselves, every vice to their enemies. With psychological adroitness no less sharply honed than his ethical insight, the prophet took advantage of popular prejudice. He began his preachment by attacking all of ancient Israel's enemies, listing them one by one, cataloguing their national sins, reciting the specific punishments God would visit upon them. Then, having whetted his listeners' appetites, having aroused their frenzy over the relationship between sin and punishment for other peoples, he dramatically shifted gears, zeroing in on themselves as prime targets for divine retribution:

> For three transgressions of Israel,
> For four, I will not revoke it:
> . . . I will slow your movements
> As a wagon is slowed
> When it is full of grain.
> Flight shall fail the swift,
> The strong shall find no strength,
> And the warrior shall not save his life.

Here we come closest to the essence of prophetic genius. Amos deplores evil everywhere, but most sharply and especially among his kinfolk. After all, he is one of them. He is preaching to them, not to the people of Syria or Gaza or Edom.

So I have often envisaged Amos speaking today to the Senate Foreign Relations Committee. Or the American Legion. He would never bypass the international hypocrisies and perfidies of other nations. But neither would he allow us to hide our own delinquencies beneath a camouflage of theirs. For three transgressions of the United States, for four: for supporting dictatorships throughout the world; for subverting legitimate governments that refuse to guarantee the properties and profits of our large corporations; for aiding and abetting the assassination of leaders overseas; for urging other nations to resist terrorism while we ourselves were surreptitiously selling arms to Iran, a principal sponsor of international terrorism—for all these transgressions, history will not revoke its verdict. Unless we acknowledge our sins and correct them, disaster will surely come to the world, including ourselves!

This, I am positive, is what Amos would say to us. And this is precisely what I have tried to voice. It is because I see myself as a spiritual heir of Amos that I was among the first American clergy-people consistently and vigorously to criticize American policy in Vietnam. I preached against it, signed petitions opposing it, sponsored meetings and marches protesting it.

Which brings us to the American Legion Crosscup-Pishon Post. In September 1965, Post leadership invited me to be one of three recipients of its annual Good Government Award. I was to share this honor on 26 January 1966 with Richard Cardinal Cushing and Episcopal Bishop Anson Phelps Stokes, Jr. All three of us accepted, and the Legion published posters bearing our pictures. Five weeks in advance of the awards dinner, I joined fifty-seven other national leaders in sponsoring a peace march in Washington to criticize United States policy in Vietnam. The following day the Legion advised me that their invitation was being withdrawn. New posters were printed, now displaying the photographs of only the other two awardees. There presumably the matter was expected to rest.

But it didn't. I immediately called a press conference to expose the entire episode. The heart of the statement I released there read as follows:

> The right of responsible dissent is a cornerstone of American democratic freedom. I joined a distinguished company of religious leaders and Nobel Prize winners, of university professors and philosophers, of statesmen and

war veterans, in exercising the precious privilege of dissent. I respect those whose views differ from my own. This is the American way—the only American way. The claim that patriotism demands at all times an uncritical acceptance of government policy is a characteristic of dictatorship, not of democracy. It is far more compatible with "Heil Hitler" than with "I pledge allegiance. . . . "

The Legion Post commander has said: "We couldn't give him an award when he was doing something opposite to the American Legion position." It is apparent, then, that this is not a Good Government Award; it is an Agree-with-the-American-Legion Award.

The Legion wasn't finished yet with its poster-printing. Bishop Stokes, while making it clear that he did not agree with my views on Vietnam, nevertheless staunchly upheld my right of dissent and "regretfully" refused to accept his part of the prize. Cardinal Cushing spoke kindly of Bishop Stokes and myself: "For years they have been in the fore-front of every worthwhile effort to make the moral message felt in the marketplace of men. They have combined to a unique degree piety and patriotism." Despite which, the Cardinal continued, "Whatever judgments are now being made concerning the other recipients are beyond my consideration in expressing heartfelt appreciation for the award to be conferred upon me."

Cushing's statement surprised me all the more because he had through the years been a good friend to me personally as well as to the Jewish community and had joined his colleagues of the clergy many times in support of liberal causes. Enter poster number three, with one picture, one name. A prized page in my scrapbook contains the three posters, side by side. An editor of *Time* commenced his letter to me with, " . . . and then there was one . . . "

Since my views on Vietnam had never been a secret,

90

why did the Legion invite me in the first place? The ostensible reason was a sermon I had given on Iwo Jima. Under circumstances to be described later, it had achieved a considerable degree of notoriety. In view of the fact, however, that this sermon had been delivered more than twenty years earlier and had nothing to do with good government, the question remains: why had I really been invited? The answer is simple. The Legion was playing the well-worn con game of selecting three prominent individuals of three faiths, in the expectation of thereby multiplying the number of people who would purchase tickets for its dinner. They themselves later acknowledged that in place of the eighteen hundred persons they had confidently expected, less than three hundred actually attended.

Why did I agree to accept the award? Not quite so simple an answer here. Having done my homework better than they did theirs, I was well aware of the differences on American foreign and military policy between the Legion and myself. While I had scarcely anticipated so clumsy an error, I knew that the choice of a person like myself would inevitably cause the Post great embarrassment. Frankly, I didn't mind that at all. I had another motive. This was, remember, near the end of the period of Joseph McCarthy's horrendous terrorism. I felt honored to have been one of his targets and to know that a dossier bearing my name was in the files of the House Committee on Un-American Activities. To me this was evidence that I had not entirely defaulted on my prophetic duties. Still, one never knew when or whence the next attack might come. There had been some grumbling within the congregation about my "radicalism." Though I must add in all fairness that not once did the Board of Trustees try to limit my freedom. In any event, it couldn't hurt to have the implicit endorsement of so reactionary a group as the

8

Pacifist

I wore my 2 percent pin with pride, almost defiantly. The idea had originated with Albert Einstein, who was convinced that if only 2 percent of the adult males in every nation would resolutely refuse to fight, war would be impossible.

Through my years of high school, college, graduate study and even into the initial stage of my professional life, absolute pacifism was one of my most cherished—and I thought inviolate—ideals. I joked (some joke!) that in the event of another war, I had already selected my prison cell. I read avidly every pacifist tome I could find and argued the position with zeal.

Why was the very thought of war so utterly repugnant to me? In part, I suppose, because in childhood and adolescence I was of less than average weight and size. I loved fighting with words, turned pale at the thought I might have to defend myself with violence. My more important reason—or rationalization?—was that I took literally the imperative emphasis of Judaism on peace. I identified with Isaiah:

> Woe to those who go down to Egypt for help
> And rely upon horses!
> They have put their trust in abundance of chariots,
> In vast numbers of riders,
> And they have not turned to the Holy One of Israel,
> They have not sought the Lord.

And with Zechariah: "Not by might, nor by power, but by My spirit—said the Lord of Hosts!"

Born in 1910, I was too young during World War I to sense much of what was going on. I do remember the fascination and pride with which I listened later to my two closest uncles telling of their experiences in the army and navy. The fascination, the pride . . . and the fear. What would I do if ever I had to be a soldier or sailor? This dread was reinforced a few years afterward when I was repulsed by gory photographs of battlefield atrocities. In any event, for whichever reasons, war became for me the ultimate immorality, to be shunned at all cost.

The degree of my pacifism can best be measured by a sermon I preached early in World War II, after Hitler's massive initial victories and during the interval when we Americans were debating whether or not to enter the conflict. In it, I said—more correctly, I shouted: "If we do nothing else, we *must* stay out of this war . . . It shouldn't be necessary to convince you that I hate Hitler and want desperately to see him defeated. You will know how I want America to stay out of this war if I tell you from the bottom of my heart that, much as I want Hitler to lose, I want us to stay out of the war even if he seems to be winning."

I can still see an elderly German widower who was sitting on the center aisle. I can still hear the snort with which he reacted to my perfervid but foolish words. To his everlasting credit, he neither walked out nor resigned from the congregation. During the months and years that followed, I learned two invaluable lessons from this experience: first, to respect those members of congregations who cherish their rabbis' freedom of the pulpit enough to tolerate even such extremist views as I had urged; second, never again to consider any belief or view of mine to be beyond all possibility of change.

The man who so publicly proclaimed that he preferred pacifism to a Hitler victory eventually became a Marine Corps chaplain. Why? What made me, after the most excruciating moral dilemma of my life, renounce my pacifism and apply for a military commission? Several things. Hitler's nefarious ambition to exterminate the entire Jewish people had become transparent. I couldn't possibly accede to so ugly and evil a price for my pacifism. Young men whom I had taught and confirmed were being drafted. I had no right to hide behind my rabbinic exemption or to leave them away from home and in combat bereft of religious leadership. Finally, I felt a heavy sense of responsibility to my colleagues.

At that time the Central Conference of American Rabbis had no drafting authority. We did establish a voluntary system of priorities, listing our members in the following categories: single men, married men without children, married men with one child, with two children, etc. As the military called for more Jewish chaplains, we proceeded through our unofficial lists, advising rabbis that more chaplains were needed and we had reached them. Each was then free to make his own decision, on the basis of conscience and conviction. For me to refuse would obviously mean that someone with more right to remain exempt than I would be notified next. Or that we rabbis as a whole would renege on our responsibility to young Jewish men who most probably would need us more than ever before. So, in the waning days of 1942, I applied.

As the threat of nuclear catastrophe has loomed larger and more ominously on the horizon since 1945, I have been increasingly tempted to return to my ertswhile absolute pacifism. Yet I see that now as a puristic position that cannot avail. It is too late—after a lifetime of heavy smoking has produced lung cancer—to resist surgery as a wastage of blood. The way to deal with cancer is to prevent it; the time is long before it appears. Judaism teaches that the sword comes into the world because of the denial of justice and delay in achieving justice. We approach the perilous brink of war due to a multitude of factors—psychological, political, economic, ethical; because we have allowed monstrous immoralities to fester instead of eradicating them. The only way to prevent the ultimate explosion is to avoid or erase the iniquities that cause it. I am afraid that once these iniquities have mounted, not even the refusal to fight by ten times Einstein's quota will help, especially as war becomes more and more fiendishly technological, with fewer combatants producing many more casualties.

Does Judaism justify the claim of conscientious objection to war? Clearly it is not a faith that compels that stance. Many times, however—during the Vietnam era more than at the time of World War II—I was called upon by draft boards to authenticate the assertion by young Jews that Judaism validated their refusal to participate in military activity. I could do so with clean conscience.

I knew that Jewish tradition describes two kinds of war, *milchemet chovah*, compulsory or obligatory war, and *milchemet r'shut*, optional war. Every Jew is obligated to participate in the first. But *milchemet chovah* is restricted to such conflicts as that against the ancient Amalekites, the first nation to attack our ancestors when they departed from Egypt, a perennially implacable enemy who attempted time and again to exterminate the Jewish people.

World War II, fought in large part against Hitler, was a *milchemet chovah*. The defense of Israel against Arab aggression is a *milchemet chovah*. In such a war, according to

Jewish law, every Jew must fight, for defeat would mean our annihilation. Every other kind of conflict is for Judaism a *milchemet r'shut*, an optional war. Each individual Jew retains his personal right to participate in or refrain from such a war. For the American Jew, seeking to guide his citizenship according to Jewish ethical imperatives, there would be the same valid distinction between two kinds of war and the same obligation to participate where American survival is at stake. Knowing that helped me when conscientious objectors or draft boards came to me for advice.

It helped me also to remember that Jewish tradition surrounds every military effort with a whole complex of restriction and restraint. There is, for example, the twentieth chapter of Deuteronomy, which offers an amazing manual of combat. It orders that before entering upon a battle, the priest must address the assembled troops to encourage them. "Then the officials shall address the troops as follows, 'Is there anyone who has built a new house but has not dedicated it? Let him go back to his home, lest he die in battle and another dedicate it. Is there anyone who has planted a vineyard but has never harvested it? Let him go back to his home, lest he die in battle and another initiate it. Is there anyone who has spoken for a woman in marriage, but who has not yet married her? Let him go back to his home, lest he die in battle and another marry her. . . . Is there anyone afraid and disheartened? Let him go back to his home, lest the courage of his comrades flag like his.' "

Centuries after this instruction had been written, Rabbi Akiva noticed a redundancy: two adjectives are used in the original Hebrew. *Yaray* means either *afraid* or *disheartened*. Why was it necessary to use also the term *rach ha-lay-vav*? Akiva suggested that *rach ha-lay-vav* should be translated not as *disheartened* but as *tender-hearted*, and that it refers to a man who is a "hero among heroes, powerful among the most powerful, but who at the same time is merciful." The best twentieth-century American translation of *rach-ha-lay-vav* I can think of is *conscientious objector*. He too is exempt from combat.

Where does this leave us today? What can Judaism say to its distressed and perplexed young people who agonize now over draft registration, tomorrow, God forbid, over involuntary military induction? Unlike such denominations as the Quakers and Mennonites, our tradition does not force absolute pacifism upon its adherents. Each Jew is franchised to decide for himself whether a given conflict is *milchemet chovah* or *milchemet r'shut*, and to act accordingly. Both the conscientious objector and the person who agrees to serve in the military can claim the endorsement of their religious heritage. Jewish faith and law clearly support the individual who claims on religious grounds that he or she cannot participate in war.

Both the Reform and Conservative rabbinic bodies have attested to this. The Central Conference of American Rabbis has proclaimed: "Conscientious objection to military service is in accordance with the highest interpretation of Judaism." The Rabbinical Assembly agrees: "We recognize the right of the conscientious objector to claim exemption from military service in any war in which he cannot give his moral assent, and we pledge ourselves to support him in his determination to refrain from any participation in it."

The second of these statements exceeds the first in justifying, at least by implication, selective as well as general conscientious objection. Which means to say, one who doesn't necessarily repudiate all war as a matter of principle may nonetheless judge a particular war to be unworthy of moral approval. What may be merely implied here was made explicit and direct on other occasions. The Central Conference in 1966, the Rabbinical Assembly in 1968 both appealed to the United States government to accept the pleas of those who did not conscientiously object to all war but found it morally repugnant to serve in Vietnam.

There are no simple, easy answers for the Jew on conscientious objection. Except for those who deliberately distort it, or use it to validate their own preconceived purposes, Judaism doesn't offer simple, easy answers to any of life's crucial dilemmas. On the one hand, we have been faithful, loyal, patriotic citizens of every nation that has hosted us, providing more than our share of military support when such nations were engaged in war. We have also recognized how essential it is for citizens to obey the law, for without law there is anarchy and anarchy means chaos. On the other hand, in words adopted by the Union of American Hebrew Congregations, we know that "many of our greatest prophets and rabbis are revered precisely because they placed the imperatives of conscience above the dictates of the state."

In the end, Judaism gives even higher priority to responsibly motivated conscience than to government and law. This was recognized and enunciated by all three religious branches of Judaism in a memorable pronouncement issued by the Synagogue Council of America: "Respect for law is deeply ingrained in the texture of Judaism. . . . It is clear that no system of law is possible where each (person) is obliged to obey only those laws that correspond to his (her) views.

"At the same time, Judaism considers each individual personally responsible before God for his actions. No (person) who violates the eternal will of the Creator can escape responsibility by pleading that he acted as an agent of another, whether that other be an individual or the state.

It is therefore possible, under unusual circumstances, for an individual to find himself compelled by conscience to reject the demands of a human law which . . . appears to conflict with the demand made on him by a higher law."

The Midrash comes as close as any source to expressing the essential thought of Judaism on this matter. It observes that as Jacob prepared to rejoin his brother Esau, according to the description in Genesis he "was greatly afraid and distressed." An ancient rabbi expanded on this simple statement: "Are not fear and distress identical? The meaning is that 'he was afraid' lest he be slain, 'and distressed' lest he should slay. For he thought: 'If he prevails against me, will he not slay me? While if I am stronger than he, will I not slay him?'"

Golda Meir, when she was Prime Minister of Israel, echoed the Patriarch's plaint when she said: "We can forgive the Arabs for killing us; we can never forgive them for forcing us to kill them."

Jacob's dilemma was that of every young Jew with whom I have agonized—or may yet agonize—over conscientious objection to war. My own decision, for myself, had been far too excruciating to authorize my intervention into another's conscience. I can offer no panaceas, no promises, no guarantees. I can only share each person's anguished inner struggle toward a decision with which he or she can live. And assure that person that Judaism accepts and supports those who refuse to kill.

9
Chaplain

Back to 1942.

I applied for a commission in the Navy, explaining my preference facetiously by saying that my wife preferred me in blue, that I wanted to eat off a white tablecloth, that I didn't want to carry a knapsack or dig foxholes. So I became a Marine Corps chaplain, wearing only khaki and green, never blue; there were no tablecloths of any color; I carried a knapsack and dug foxholes.

Hard as it is even for me to believe now, in 1942 I was so naive in military matters that I didn't even know the Marine Corps was part of the Navy until, just before graduation from the United States Naval Training School for Chaplains, I found myself the first Jewish chaplain in American history assigned to Marine Corps duty. Once in, I went where I was assigned: to assist the famous William A. Maguire of "Praise the Lord and pass the ammunition" fame in San Diego; to become Assistant Division Chaplain and Jewish Chaplain of the Fifth Marine Division; to train with them at Camp Pendleton in California, then Camp Tarawa on the island of Hawaii; to participate in the conquest of Iwo Jima; and after V-J Day, to waste time for two months doing virtually nothing at Camp Sampson in upstate New York while collecting enough "points" for discharge.

On the day of my return to civilian life, I said that I wouldn't take a million dollars for the military experience

Conducting Passover seder, United States Marine Corps Base, San Diego, California, Spring 1944.

but wouldn't willingly repeat it for five million. Never before or since have I felt so important and needed by others. Even prior to combat, the Jewish chaplain was a symbol of status and security for his men. At every instance of suspected anti-Semitism, they ran to him immediately as the only authority on whom they could rely.

I never failed to pursue such appeals. If my investigation convinced me that the suspicion of prejudice was unwarranted, my task was to explain the facts to the man involved. Where the evidence justified his charge, I became, so to speak, his attorney.

One incident remains inscribed on my mind indelibly. A sergeant returned to his tent one night drunk. There he encountered a half-dozen men. Staggering over to the single Jew in their midst, he slurred the following through lips almost immobilized by intoxication: "One good thing Hitler has done is to kill Jews. The only trouble is he didn't get all of you. When I get back to the States, I'd like to finish you yids off there."

The next morning, after verifying the facts by talking to others who were present, I consulted with the sergeant's Protestant chaplain and the two of us approached him. We were surprised to find a pleasant, freckle-faced farm boy from Iowa, a hero at that. He had been at Tarawa, had helped pull 75 mm. guns to within a few dozen yards of Japanese machine gun positions to blast them away. Why did he say what he did the night before? He mumbled his answer with bowed, dejected head: "I'm ashamed of myself. I don't really feel that way. As far as I'm concerned, Jews are like anybody else—some good, some bad. I guess I just had too much beer and shot my mouth off."

I heard this kind of defense many times. A man claims to harbor no hate in his heart. He succumbs to the influence of alcohol. And the first thing his unbridled tongue does, by instinct, is to abuse the nearest Jew! My Protestant colleague nodded vigorous assent as I said to the sergeant, "You can't hide behind alcohol. When you're drunk and your inhibitions are down, that's precisely when you're likely to say what you really mean. One more case like that, I promise to take to higher authority." After a while I could recite the words by rote.

From one extreme to the other: the ex-absolute pacifist put in for a revolver. True, the Geneva Convention forbade physicians and chaplains from carrying weapons; this by way of recognizing our special status as non-combatants and granting us immunity from assault. I knew that, the League of Nations knew it, all governments knew it. But would a desperate Japanese soldier carrying out a banzai attack on Iwo know it? Even if he did, would he bother to observe medical or religious insignia before firing his carbine or plunging his bayonet into our flesh? I didn't want to find out. Therefore—like all our division's doctors and chaplains—I obtained a revolver, learned how to clean and maintain it, went regularly to the firing range to practice using it.

I never had to fire it in combat. Would I have done so if directly attacked? I think so, but don't really know for sure. Thank God, the choice was never forced upon me.

The saddest hours I had ever known occurred on the day when, in preparation for my being shipped overseas, I put my family on a train headed eastward. We spent the afternoon together on a lovely lagoon in Los Angeles. I was only partly successful in suppressing my tears as I bade them farewell. The time between their departure and my midnight train for San Francisco was filled with the empty motions of eating dinner and sitting through a meaningless movie. Because group sharing of taxis was mandatory then under wartime traffic congestion, I shared a cab with three businessmen who were on their way home from a trade convention.

Oblivious of my uniform, they complained endlessly about the difficulties imposed on them by the war: hotel rooms were all but impossible to obtain . . . service and food in even the best restaurants were abominable . . . government regulations were a most annoying obstacle to earning the proper amount of profit. So on and on, until I finally exploded, "I don't know who you guys are, but I want you to know how sorry I am over your troubles. I just kissed my wife and children good-bye, not knowing whether I'll ever see them again. Tomorrow I'm being flown overseas, sooner or later into combat. But your plight really touches me; my heart bleeds for you."

The ensuing silence was eloquent. I'm afraid I was less than gracious in refusing their embarrassed invitation to be their guest for drinks while waiting for our respective trains.

The closer we approached combat, the more immediate and important my duties as a chaplain became.

The night before D-day, as our attack-transport slowly crept through murky darkness toward Iwo Jima, I was asked to speak to all the men on board through the ship's public address system. My files still include the notes, nervously scratched on onion-skin paper, from which I spoke. What did I say? "Men, I'm going to be speaking in these next few minutes quite as much to myself as to you. We're in this thing together. The same fears and doubts and high hopes which fill your hearts tonight are in mine." I then proceeded to spell out the spiritual weapons that I as a chaplain could add to the physical arms and ammunition with which we would hit the beach the next morning. The love of parents and wives who were with us despite the many intervening miles. The pride each of us possessed— pride not only in the United States Marine Corps but in ourselves. "It's you and I who will win this campaign with our tanks and planes, not they with us. . . . You may fire the shot that will break the enemy's back. You may, by your own example of courage, give strength to fifty other men and they to five hundred more."

And finally, faith. Faith in ourselves, in each other, in all those who supported us. And, of course, faith in God. "Faith that in and above and beyond this terrible struggle there is a great unseen Power that works with us if we work with It, a Power that makes for righteousness and insures the triumph of righteousness."

I offered them no guarantees. Only hope. "God bless you! May we win our objective with the least possible loss. May we carry through, each of us so that he never need be ashamed of himself. And may we return speedily to our dearest ones to carry on with them in peace our struggle for the rights of common people everywhere. Amen." Months later suvivors of Iwo told me how these words had helped them.

Both the Protestant chaplain and I had been assigned cabins that night for personal consultations. By the time I reached mine after concluding my address, a long line of Marines stood before the entrance. At first I was puzzled by the fact that there appeared to be many more men than I had identified as Jews during the seven weeks we had been maneuvering and practicing since leaving Hilo. The mystery was immediately solved. A number of those who impatiently awaited me had already visited my colleague; some of the others would reverse the order, going from me to him. They were taking no chances, carrying with them the next day crucifixes or crosses from him, *mezuzot* from me, pocket Bibles from both of us. No one could fairly fault them at that moment for acting more out of fundamental fright than from adult religion.

Weeks later I often instigated discussion with my Jewish Marines on two levels of reasons why they might have wanted to carry Bibles with them into combat. Level one: childish superstition. The little volume in knapsack or pocket might serve as a magic talisman, protecting its bearer from harm. Or it might even stop a bullet that would otherwise have penetrated human flesh. There were, indeed, a few such bizarre cases reported in the press. Level two: mature faith. The Bible he carried could remind a Jewish Marine of his identification with a historic people that had survived many crises comparable to that which now confronted him. It could also symbolize that people's faith, and his own, in God as a Power that enables us to surmount worries and fears that might otherwise crush us. The night before D-day, I tried to meet each man where he was; this was not the time for theological instruction. My desire to help my men grow from where they were to where they should be, from superstition to genuine faith—that could await a less frightening and more propitious moment.

I doubt that a single one of us enjoyed more than a few snatches of fitful sleep the night before D-day. Because the U.S.S. *Deuel* immediately became an auxiliary hospital ship after its combat troops had left, higher authority had decided that I could serve more usefully for the first two days by remaining on board. At the first glimpse of dawn on 19 February, I went topside with the men, spent the morning walking back and forth on deck, talking to those who awaited their turn to go over the side. We had, all of us, practiced clambering down a cargo net so many times that this once dificult operation had become all but automatic. But this was different. This time we knew that more than a few of us would never board ship again.

I remember especially two of the kids to whom I spoke at length that morning. One was about eighteen years old. The content of our conversation faded from my memory years ago. But I recall the letter he wrote me about two months afterward from a naval hospital in which he was recuperating from battle wounds. He thanked me profusely for the encouragement he said I had given him at the ship's rail, said he doubted whether he could have "made it" without my words.

Then there was a young pharmacist's mate. I've never seen any human being so uncontrollably terrified in my life. His eyes were red with sleeplessness and fear. Not only his lips and hands, literally his entire body trembled. What could I possibly say? Only that I understood his fear and shared it, that there would have been something abnormal about both of us if we felt other than we did. Whatever my words, he managed somehow to do what he had to and forty-eight hours later, when my turn came, I did the same.

For the first three horrible days after landing, I neither saw nor heard of him. On the fourth day, his name was on the list of men I was burying in our Division Cemetery. Later, by talking to some of those who had been with him when he was killed, I was able to piece together what had happened. In the midst of a furious Japanese counterattack, he had taken refuge in a shell-hole. From another hole, twenty or thirty yards away, he heard the pitiful moans of a Marine who had been hit and was crying for help. If my young friend had stayed where he was, he might well have survived. He did not stay where he was. He had been trained to save life, and a nearby life needed saving. He crawled out of his shelter to render medical aid . . . shrapnel from the next shell caught him . . . he was killed.

Not long after the last of our ship's troops had left, the first casualties were brought back. Torn flesh . . . broken bones . . . shattered minds: every man demanded and deserved immediate attention. Neither the doctors nor I, the only chaplain still on board, knew where to turn first. I, who had always felt faint at the sight of blood, who would still turn pale if blood flowed in my presence now, stood by an improvised surgical table, holding a young casualty's hand while hunks of shrapnel were being dug out of his knee. The boy's face was pale with pain; his teeth had punctured his lips with blood; his fingernails dug into my palm so deeply that marks were still visible hours later. But each time I inquired about the pain, his grim answer was the same, "Okay, padre!"

This was only the beginning. Later, on the island itself, I saw blood enough to float a yacht. Why didn't I black out then? Perhaps because I was needed; perhaps because I would have been ashamed to distract medical attention from those who had already suffered too much; perhaps because, when horror becomes wholesale, our emotions are desensitized to protect us.

A few days after our return to Hawaii I wrote the following to my sister, in answer to a letter in which she had apparently commented on my Iwo behavior:

You know, it's strange reading that you think I was strong on Iwo. Somehow I don't impress me that way at all. The feeling one has in combat is hard to describe. All I know is that no one was weaker or more utterly frightened than I on the way up to Iwo, and that now in recollection I wonder whether I was really able to go through the things the papers say I did. During our actual days on the island no one had time or energy to ask questions or to analyze whether he was weak or strong. It was almost like being under the influence of anesthesia: you had a job to do, so you did it. It was as simple as that. You didn't dare sit or stand in one place too long because you didn't want a sniper to get a "bead" on you. So you just kept rushing around, I suspect quite as much to get away from yourself as to avoid the snipers. Now in retrospect some of the things I had very little trouble living through bother me more than they did then. But whatever you do, don't credit me with being strong in combat; no one but a fool is. The rest of us just acted like a bunch of marionettes whose strings were being skillfully manipulated.

Combat itself was the most unspeakably horrendous hell I have ever known or could possibly imagine. Five weeks assumed the dimensions of five years. I remember waving to a red-headed major as his landing craft moved away from our ship toward its pre-landing rendezvous. The next time I saw him was about three weeks later on the island; his hair had literally turned white! The effect on our emotions and nerves, while of course less visible, was more devastating and permanent.

Despite the most intensive pre-combat bombardment in military history—nearly ninety days of aerial observation and assault preceded the landing on Iwo—many gross mistakes in military intelligence complicated our task and increased our casualties. The volcanic ash of the island was so coal-black that our green-and-sand colored camouflage made us more rather than less conspicuous. The grade we had to ascend from beach to air strip under terrifying counterattack was much steeper than we had been told. The soil was too shifting to hold our heavier vehicles. There were many more caves, hence many more Japanese survivors of our bombardment, than we had anticipated; the number of defensive troops still alive when we landed was twice what we had been led to believe.

The day before we hit the beach, we were told to expect approximately 700 deaths per Marine division. On that basis, we in the Fifth MarDiv planned a cemetery to hold 900 bodies. When we left the island after thirty-five days of combat, 2,280 men had been buried in our cemetery, with several hundred others missing in action.

Enemy intelligence seemed to be better than ours. Imagine the effect on our morale—steaming closer and closer to Iwo, the very day before our attack—as we listened to Tokyo Rose broadcasting, with uncanny accuracy, which beaches we intended to hit, which of our units were involved, how many men were in each. At that moment most of us, had we possessed the power, would have opted for reversing the course of our convoys and sailing away.

How a single one of us left Iwo alive is a miracle. Something like seventy to eighty thousand Americans were crowded into an area of eight square miles; no one will ever know the number of Japanese troops in and under the same surface. There were no rear areas for respite or rest. Every inch was a front line. I stood once talking to a Marine not more than ten yards away; a sniper's bullet struck and instantly killed him. I awakened one morning to find a jagged piece of shrapnel, about a foot long, on the very brink of my foxhole. Had it carried another two inches, I would not be writing this or any other book.

At one point the accuracy of enemy artillery saved us. It was my first night on the island. Several Japanese forward observers equipped with radios, hidden in a partially sunken barge, were directing their gunners' fire on one of our LSTs as it was being unloaded. So effective were their instructions and the shelling that followed that eleven consecutive salvos landed precisely on their target. Fifty yards from the LST were a hundred drums of gasoline and ammunition already unloaded from previous vessels. Had only a single shell missed by even close to fifty yards, the entire left flank of our beach would have been obliterated!

Leading first Jewish religious service during combat on Iwo Jima, Feb-

Much of my time on Iwo was spent in the Division cemetery. Because often it was impossible to know the religion of men who had been killed—there were times when all we were burying was a burlap sack only partly filled with flesh and bones—it was necessary at all times to have a Catholic, a Protestant, and a Jewish chaplain on hand. And I was the Division's only Jewish chaplain. I was in the cemetery when the American flag first flew on top of Mount Suribachi—not the dramatic flag-raising later posed for Rosenthal's famous photograph, but the original hoisting of a small flag on a thin pipe. By coincidence I raised my eyes from the mass grave in which I was standing just in time to see the symbol of a victory that had yet to be fully won. Never since have I witnessed an American flag fluttering in the wind without reliving that scene.

So many unforgettable moments and men! How do I choose now to write about some without doing unforgivable injustice to others? Like the lad I watched for three hours one afternoon in a Corps Evacuation Hospital Tent where I was waiting for one of my boys who had been badly wounded to regain consciousness. The duty corpsman could not have been older than seventeen, no fuzz yet on his face or hair on his chest. He was a boy moving among men, men who had been seriously hurt. Yet he was an angel of mercy: hurrying with steady self-assurance from patient to patient; carefully taking a pulse here, tenderly lifting a head there, patting a cheek, holding a hand, mopping a feverish brow. Where did this boy, who should have been bending over school books, not broken bodies—where did he get such strength?

In a similar setting, there was Don Fox, a good friend of mine, one of our division photographers. On a Saturday afternoon, word came to me over the field telephone that Don had been hit in the head by a sniper and was in a battalion aid station. In quick succession, I barely missed him at several such stations, finally catching up with him at a beach evacuation hospital. The brain surgeon told me immediately there was no hope. I spent the next two hours in a sweaty tent with Don, though he never knew it because he never regained consciousness. His face haunted me for months, a sweet, boyish face—eyes horribly blackened, throat so desperately gasping for breath, precious life's blood flowing so freely. There was nothing I could do for him except just sit there, pray, watch a fine young friend die. And very little I could do later for his grieving parents.

Just before blackout one night, I received a letter from Herman Podzeba's wife. She had given birth to a baby girl, their first child. Because the Red Cross was unable to clear cables to men in active combat, she had written to me, asking that I communicate the good news to her husband. Early the next morning, I started to do so. Herman had recently been transferred to another unit, making it difficult to find him. I finally tracked him down—a corpse awaiting burial. He never knew he had become a father.

What enabled us to survive such unending horror? In part, the fact that we had no choice: there was no place to run, no way to escape. Also, the combat anesthesia I have already described: the full measure of what we were seeing and hearing did not strike us until later. And also, our sense of humor. Yes, believe it or not, even in the midst of indescribable heartache and pain, we found ourselves occasionally able to laugh.

One noon about a dozen of us squatted around a regimental command post, enjoying—or suffering—our lunch of K rations and sardines. Suddenly we heard the sinister sputter of a grenade. Knives, crackers, mess gear, and Marines all scattered in every direction, waiting tensely for the explosion. There was none. A hysterically laughing chaplain's clerk explained what had happened. Tired of culinary drabness, he had hit upon the ingenious idea of varying it with grilled cheese. Putting a can of cheese on the fire to melt, he had forgotten only one thing: to pierce the tin first with a few holes. When the heated can burst its seams, three unanticipated events occurred simultaneously: the hapless chef was sprayed with a coating of thick, gooey cheese; twelve men ranging in rank from private to lieutenant-colonel moved faster than they ever had before; and to our American arsenal of secret weapons was added a new one—the cheese grenade.

It was common knowledge in the Fifth Marine Division that ice cream was my favorite food; it still is. In a moment of rashness before we hit the Iwo beach, I bet my senior chaplain that somehow I would manage to find ice cream even in combat. Four weeks later I had not succeeded. What to do? Suddenly, inspiration struck: a major hospital ship lay anchored about a half-mile offshore. It did not take long to convince the boss that there had to be Jewish casualties aboard and that a Jewish chaplain should visit them. So, with official authorization, I commandeered a small landing craft, visited the Jewish men who were recuperating from serious wounds, brought them whatever comfort I could, and returned to my Senior with a note from the ship commissary's Chief Petty Officer attesting to the fact that, after completing my visits, I had enjoyed a luscious dish of chocolate ice cream.

On another occasion one of our advancing platoons captured a number of Japanese military items, among them a bugle. Our men were still under fire; the enemy surrounded them on three sides; carbines, theirs and ours, still snapped out their staccato syllables. Suddenly, sounded from one of our foxholes on the captured bugle, we heard, of all improbable calls, those for liberty and movies!

115

It was said during the war that there were no atheists in foxholes. Rubbish! There were just as many atheists there as elsewhere, but even an atheist can be so frightened as to gamble on anything that might save him. With very few exceptions, those who didn't believe in God before Iwo didn't believe in God after Iwo; they probably didn't really believe in God on Iwo, but why take chances? They would have prayed to Santa Claus or the devil if someone had told them that either could help. I learned in combat that most of us change neither our faith nor our basic nature under the stress of emergency. Or, for that matter, as we grow older. We just become more obviously and pronouncedly what we always were.

I learned also that much of battlefield courage is almost mechanical. We moved about as robots, automatically performing the motions that had been programmed into us. There is, believe me, more heroism in civilian hospitals—among patients and their loved ones, among nurses and physicians and friends—more deliberate heroism by far than in combat.

One of my most frightening moments took place after the greatest part of our military operation had been completed and we were preparing to leave Iwo. The holiday of Passover would commence two days after we were scheduled to turn the island over to army units for occupation. Twenty or more ships, anchored a short distance off shore, would take us back to Hawaii for recuperation and retraining. I would be on only one of them, but Jews on all the others would need the Passover *seder* service as they had never needed it before. It was my responsibility to ensure that each ship, before it sailed, carried the necessary supplies.

So, on a sunny, windy day—after my sergeant and I had packed a carton weighing perhaps seven or eight pounds for each ship—we commandeered a small landing craft and set out on our mission of delivery. The only way to carry a carton aboard was to climb a Jacob's ladder, clutching each rung of the ladder with one hand, grasping the carton under the other arm. As I thus valiantly—and overconfidently?—struggled up my final Jacob's ladder of the day, a gust of wind lifted the ladder and me several yards away from the ship's side, swayed me back and forth precariously, then twisted around so that I was caught between ladder and ship facing outward. It sounds humorous now; there wasn't anything funny about it then. I am not known for kinetic dexterity; I wish I had a movie to establish just how I managed to deliver my package and save my skin.

A word about the emotional price of war: the stress didn't really hit me fully until the day we left Iwo. I couldn't afford the luxury of feeling it before then. An hour or two after boarding the ship that was to take us back to Hawaii, it was dinnertime. I sat down in the ward-room at a table covered with a white cloth, a black waiter approached to place a bowl of steaming soup before me—and I burst into the most uncontrollable explosion of tears in my whole life. Everything I had somehow managed to absorb for five weeks finally caught up with me. In the days that followed, my spirit and psyche came closer to breaking than at any time before or since. Thank God, memory has been kind to me. I suffered only two horrifying combat nightmares in the weeks that followed; some men were never able to shake them. As the years have passed, increasingly my wartime experiences have receded to the point where I sometimes feel as if they were incidents I had read about rather than horrors I had felt in the very marrow of my bones.

Yet for a long time, there were grotesque reminders. The sight of bare feet protruding from a blanket—even in the most benign of settings—evoked nightmarish memories of corpses lined up in neat rows, entirely covered except for their feet. Any unpleasant or earthy odor—of cattle, horses, perspiration—made the nerve endings of my nostrils vibrate again with the stench of decaying bodies. After a while, even these stubborn stains began mercifully to fade.

I recall them now only on the rare occasions when I have reason to reread words written then. Each month or two during my tour of overseas duty, I sent a letter to my congregants at home. From Iwo on 17 March 1945, I wrote:

I've become an expert on many things in the 35 days since last I wrote to you. On fear, for instance. All kinds of fear—past, present and future. I have seen the shadowy scars of yesterday's fear—at Pearl Harbor, at Eniwetok, at Saipan and Tinian. And I have felt the real substance of today's fear and tomorrow's in my own "inners" here on Iwo.

I know the fear of awakening in the morning to learn that the ship carrying us into combat has had repeated contacts during the night with enemy submarines. I know the fear for other men's lives that fills you as you watch them leave the ship just before H hour, and the fear for your own self that strikes you with terror when your turn comes. I know the fear of squeezing yourself lower into a foxhole, every muscle and nerve trembling, while mortar shells whistle overheard and burst too close for comfort. I know the fear of hearing snipers' bullets whizz over you, of hitting the deck in nothing flat, then finding that some poor kid fifteen feet away got it through the chest. . . . I know the fear of seeing an American fighter plane burst into flames and hurtle toward the sea, of watching in literal breathlessness for an opening parachute that never came. . . . Yes, I'm now an expert on fear.

On sorrow too—more sorrow than God ever meant us to know. The sorrow of watching day after heartbreaking day as the torn and broken bodies of husbands and sons are brought—it seems in an endless stream of sacrifice—into aid stations and hospitals. The sorrow of talking one night with a fine, handsome young officer about his wife and three children, then discovering the next day that a direct mortar hit had blown him and his sergeant to bits. . . . Sometimes I have lain awake at night in my foxhole and thought there must be so much suffering and sorrow on this little island that God Himself has had to turn away. . . .

I know joy too. The joy of slipping into a fellow's foxhole and knowing by his handshake and haggard smile how much my two-minute visit means to him. Of hearing that a young lieutenant friend had saved his colonel's life the night before during a Japanese banzai attack. Of conducting the first Jewish religious service ever held on this island and of praying last night with 60 Jewish men who tramped from every direction through Iwo's stifling volcanic dust to greet the Sabbath. . . .

And I know pride—fierce, stubborn, resolute pride. . . . The pride of a young ensign who insisted that the doctors take care of everyone else first because he had "only a scratch." The "scratch"proved to be a bullet hole clean through his leg! I know the courage and pride of a hospital corpsman who continued to adminster whatever aid he could to the wounded even after both his legs had been blown off!

Yes, indeed, there was an emotional price to pay. The cost to my family, however, was far heavier than to me. Each time I wrote a letter to my wife and children, I knew that I was whole and well. Each time they read one of my letters, all they knew was that ten days before I had still been alive. My wife suddenly had to be both mother and father to our frightened children. Only a few years after the war ended, she suffered the first in an agonizing series of emotional crises from which she never really recovered. Could she have escaped these breakdowns, and the permanent hospitalization they finally caused, had it not been for the excruciating strains of war?

Ruth did her best to protect our seven-year-old son and four-year-old daughter. She could easily piece together the absence of mail from me with the lurid newspaper headlines to figure out that I was on Iwo, but thought she had successfully shielded the children. Until one day the principal of David's school on Long Island called to tell her that our boy had fainted in class. The bullets and shells being fired on Iwo inflicted lasting scars many thousands of miles away on Long Island.

One of my regular columns, written "somewhere in the Pacific" and published in the *Nassau Daily Review*, concerned such scars: "I did a lot of thinking last night about David and Judy. They happen to be my own two kiddies . . . but might just as well be the children of any other father who is away at war. My wife had written that the children were difficult to manage after I left and that they spoke of me a great deal, at times seemed almost terrified by my absence. That made me wonder whether, in our preoccupation with gorier and more spectacular losses of this war, we aren't forgetting what may prove in the long run to be an equal loss, a generation of bewildered, war-shocked children."

After describing how our son and daughter had been uprooted from home and transported more than three-thousand miles to San Diego, I continued:

> Every visit to camp meant the visible presence of war and what it might do to their daddy. Almost daily they saw

other children's fathers leaving for overseas; soon they came to understand that one day it would be their daddy's turn. It is far too easy for adults to underestimate the depth of such fears in little minds that are, respectively, not quite four and just under seven. Both children kept asking, with alarming frequency, what I would do if, when I arrived overseas, I encountered a Jap who wanted to kill me. When they learned that I was to be shipped out by plane rather than ship, one of them said, "Boy, Dad, am I glad you're going to fly. Now I know you won't drown!"

. . . In a thousand little ways the children showed signs that a nameless terror and tension had seized them. When the moment came to kiss them good-bye on the train that was to carry them back east, it was too late for easy camouflage. True, Judy may still be a little too young to understand. But David sat on the edge of his seat, almost hypnotized, and as I kissed them he whispered over and over again as if in a trance, "Good luck, Daddy . . . good luck, Daddy . . . good luck, Daddy." He must have said it at least a dozen times. The echo of his barely audible whisper is the loudest challenge I know to the conscience of an adult generation that has pulled the props out from under its children.

What can I do, dear David and darling Judy, to make up to you this terrible thing that life has done to you? You didn't ask for this war. You don't even understand it. Surely you aren't guilty of the inexcusable mistakes that caused it. But you are among its most lamentable victims. What can I do to make it right with you? I can promise that when peace comes again, nothing . . . will come before you two and the debt your daddy owes you. I can vow that after the war my chief purpose in life will be to restore some of that confident security which has been taken away from you.

So far as possible, I kept a record of every Jewish Marine I had buried on Iwo or who was reported as missing in action. A few months after returning to my civilian pulpit in Rockville Centre, I preached a sermon entitled "Your Son Did Not Die." The families of all these men living in or near the New York area were especially invited. In a sense, this was the obverse of my earlier "sermon" aboard the U.S.S. *Deuel*. Then, I had told horribly frightened men that their loved ones were with them at that very moment; now, my message to miserably bereaved parents and wives was that their husbands and sons would live within them forever. "Just as you became a part of them and were with them and gave them strength in their last moments, so tonight and for the rest of your lives they are with you and their great strength will give you strength."

I tried to transform morose dreams of the past into constructive action for the future. "Somewhere there's a miner's son just the age of your boy who never had a decent chance in life because his father was killed in a mine accident and he himself has had to slave in the mine ever since. Do something for him, and you keep your boy alive. Somewhere there's a Negro who can't be the artist or scholar he wants to be because his skin happens not to be the exact shade of yours or mine. Spend the rest of your days achieving justice and fulfillment for him, and you keep your boy alive. Somewhere there's a Jew, a young Jew like your son, who has miraculously lived through the horror of Holcaust. Keep that young Jew alive, bring him into Palestine where he can rebuild his life with dignity. Thus will you keep your son alive."

I concluded with a letter that had been handed to me before combat by a nineteen-year-old Jewish hospital apprentice who asked me to deliver it to his parents if he were killed:

> It is getting very near to that time when we shall depart on our first mission of combat. And before I leave, I have

122

Being decorated for Iwo Jima campaign, Island of Hawaii, Summer 1945.

to tell you what is and has been going on in my heart all the time that we have been separated by the broad expanse of the Pacific Ocean.

I told you when I was leaving that nothing bothered me as much as the thought of the trouble I was causing you by going away, or might cause you if I were not to return. Now that death is closer, I feel the same. I don't find the thought of death a great terror that weighs on me. I feel rather that if I were not to return, it would be you and those who love me who would have the real burden to bear, and I am writing this letter to explain why, after all, I do not think it should be regarded merely as a burden.

We make the division between life and death as if it were one of dates. But just as we sleep half our lives, so when we are awake we know that often we are only half alive. Life, in fact, is a quality rather than a quantity, and there are certain moments of life whose value seems so great that to measure them by the clock and find them to have lasted so many hours and minutes must appear trivial and meaningless. Their power is such that we cannot properly tell how long they last, for they can color all the rest of our lives, and remain a source of strength and joy. The first time I met Elaine remains with me as an instance of what I mean. If such moments could be preserved and the rest strained off, none of us could wish for anything better.

And just as these moments of joy may fill our lives, so too they may be prolonged in the experience of our friends and, exercising their power in those lives, may know a continual resurrection. Will you at least try, if I do not return (God forbid), not to let the things I have loved cause you pain, but rather increased enjoyment because I have found such joy in them. In that way the joy I had can continue to live. I cannot bear to think that if I didn't return, I should only give you sorrow. . . .

124

10

Hate

I shouldn't have been so shocked.

Even before Iwo, there were adumbrations enough to alert me had I been awake. Not at Camp Pendleton. My contacts with my colleagues in training there, except for the senior chaplain, to whom I was directly responsible, were minimal, limited to very rare staff meetings and to those occasions when protocol required that I work through chaplains assigned to specific regiments. I was a commuter, leaving camp every day at four in the afternoon to spend the evening and night with my family. Once we reached our final training camp on the island of Hawaii, however, what had been only nascent in California emerged in full bloom.

Clearly, I was not very popular among the Christian chaplains. One reason had to do with the logistics of my title and position; it may have prevailed even had I not been a Jew. In order that the one Jewish chaplain in each Marine Division might have full access to every regiment, he was automatically designated Assistant Division Chaplain and placed in Headquarters Company. This gave him status and prestige above that of the others, whose jurisdiction was in each case limited to his own regiment. For that reason I was the second highest clergyman in our Table of Organization even though I had been the last of seventeen chaplains assigned to the division. This meant, among other advantages, that for several months I lived in a relatively comfortable cabin while my colleagues were all in tents. Reason enough by itself for jealousy.

From that point on, the antagonism directed toward me was related to my disposition, my conduct, and my faith. There were the Blacks, for instance, not more than about a dozen in the entire outfit, all of them Christians. Their functions were strictly limited to serving food to the officers, ammunition to the gunners. With a disproportionate number of Marines coming from the South, the lot of those who were black was scarcely enviable. They quickly learned that there were only two chaplains in the division who gave a damn about them, who would take their complaints about discrimination seriously, and do something to defend them. Most of my Christian colleagues resented this bitterly; snide remarks were the order of the day whenever I had occasion to speak up for a Black.

I did not always wait for the black Marines to request my help. Sometimes those who needed me most had no way of reaching me. There was Jack Kelley, Jr., for instance. Someone at Headquarters Company, knowing of my interest, asked whether I knew that Jack had been given a brig sentence at the instigation of a Southern warrant officer. I investigated. It became convincingly clear that his sole offense had been a refusal to be sufficiently subservient to a white man. Within a day or two, Jack was out of the brig. He subsequently married, became a shipyard worker, lives in Oakland, California. I am still his chaplain. Across all the intervening years, no Christmas has passed without a card from him. When his mother died and Jack needed solace, he turned to me. I tried to bring him whatever written comfort could survive a distance of three thousand miles.

There were also instances of more direct and overt anti-Semitism. The Anti-Defamation League of B'nai Brith

126

had published a brief, very effective compilation of questions and answers aimed at popular misconceptions about Judaism and Jews. At about the same time, the Jewish Welfare Board issued a pamphlet detailing Jewish participation in the military history of the United States; it was entitled *Fighting for America.*

I ordered copies of both for our regimental libraries supervised by the chaplains. At a staff meeting, I made them available, asking each of my colleagues to take as many as he needed for his library. Several of them refused. One vociferously expressed his objection to both pamphlets. Having read them, he spurned the JWB collection because it "made Jews out to be perfect patriots." The ADL pamphlet was unacceptable, he said, because it stated that the Romans had crucified Jesus, while "anyone who knows anything at all knows that the Jews were guilty. If you want your Jewish boys to read this trash, give it to them yourself. I refuse to put it on the shelf for Christians to read!"

On another occasion I was on the receiving end of a barrage from three colleagues, two Catholics plus the Protestant who had rejected my library suggestions. Among the choice bits of putative knowledge conveyed to me were the following: the trouble with Washington is that too many Jews have a part in running it . . . the Lincoln Brigade, which fought Franco in Spain, consisted almost entirely of Jews, which was to be expected, since all Jews are godless Communists . . . I was a poor chaplain because I spent too much time fighting anti-Semitism, not enough teaching Judaism . . . there must be something wrong with Jews if people who, after all, aren't born prejudiced, nevertheless learn from experience not to trust Jews. As I listened, saddened and stunned into silence, a Catholic colleague, the most popular priest in the Division, sealed the encounter by describing Charles Coughlin, the notoriously anti-Semitic radio broadcaster of that time as "the greatest Catholic priest in the world. I'd kiss the ground he walks on!"

A relevant parenthesis: While we were stationed on Hawaii—both before and after Iwo Jima—I conducted two evening discussion groups, one on Mondays, the other on Wednesdays. They were open to all who were interested. Our topics centered mostly on the issues—social, ethical, political, moral—for which I believed the war was being waged. On the few occasions that we addressed ourselves to religious subjects—because all faiths were included among the regular participants—we approached the matter from the perspective of comparative religion.

In leading these groups, I committed two cardinal sins: First, I invited the Blacks I knew to join; five or six actually did. Second, in order that all sides of important issues be covered as impartially as possible, I wrote to a number of organizations for pamphlet material. The commanding general who took over after our return from Iwo sent me a message via my senior chaplain: since I had two such meetings a week, wouldn't it be a good idea, instead of mixing Whites and Blacks, to hold separate sessions for each? I sent my answer also through the good offices of my superior: I promised faithfully never to interfere with the military leadership of the division, because I didn't consider myself to be an expert in that field; it would be greatly appreciated if the general would reciprocate when it came to my area of competence. Dale Carnegie would not have approved.

My conduct on the second count pleased the general no more than on the first. For our discussions on labor relations, I wrote for informational material to several unions, including the International Longshoreman's

Union, then led by Harry Bridges, an acknowledged Communist. The fact that I also ordered pamphlets from the United States Chamber of Commerce and the National Association of Manufacturers was apparently considered irrelevant. I was a dangerous person to have around.

One afternoon, after our return from Iwo, a young Christian lieutenant in Headquarters Company, a man whom I knew only casually, asked if we could take a walk together. I was flattered and pleased. After we had left camp limits, his purpose became plain: did I know that I was being investigated by G2, the intelligence arm of the division? That every piece of mail directed to and from me was being opened and read? My informant did not have to add that he was risking court-martial and severe punishment in disclosing this to me. The tidings he brought changed my behavior in no way whatever; I continued to write my letters exactly as before, to conduct my discussion groups as I always had, to expose my men to all the information I could give them, hoping they would learn how to evaluate and to strike a realistic balance between contending views.

Some weeks later I was transferred from the Fifth Marine Division to temporary duty at Pearl Harbor, awaiting orders to return stateside. There I was able to fill in the missing informational gap. One Sunday when I was duty chaplain, my own personnel file, ordinarily locked away, was strangely left among papers to which the duty chaplain always had access. That could have been an innocent mistake; I'm more inclined to think it was the deliberate act of my new senior chaplain, who wanted me to see the file. In any event, the key endorsement of my erstwhile commanding general read, as nearly as I can remember it across the years: "There is no evidence that Lt. Gittelsohn is an actual Communist, but he favors many of the causes supported by the Communists. It is requested that he be transferred out of the Division."

I was flagrantly guilty. At that time the Communists, our military allies, favored a victory over Japan. So did I. By the way, my "punishment" for this offense was being returned to the United States and my family six months earlier than I would otherwise have been.

Did anti-Semitism play any role in this whole ugly episode? Who knows? The causes of prejudice are complicated and devious, often so organically interwoven as to defy surgical separation. I shall never know for sure the extent to which my being Jewish was a factor here.

All this in a sense is preface. The most bitterly, blatantly anti-Semitic experience I have ever endured came at the very conclusion of combat. It had to do with the sermon mentioned earlier, which I delivered at the dedication of our Fifth Marine Division Cemetery. As the time approached for us to depart Iwo, our Division Chaplain, Warren Cuthriell, began to plan the cemetery dedication. First there would be a secular ceremony, at which, of course, an address would be given by the commanding general, not the one who later requested my transfer. Then the three major faiths were to unite in a religious memorial service. As spokesman for the smallest of these religious denominations, I was invited to preach the memorial sermon. All hell broke loose at once!

Two of the Protestant chaplains waited on Chaplain Cuthriell to express their vigorous objection; it would be highly offensive for a rabbi to preach over the graves of men who were predominantly Christians. Cuthriell's immediate answer was that the right of a Jew to preach for such an occasion was precisely one of the things for which the war was being fought. That, if you please, from a Southern Baptist who had probably met no more than a dozen Jews in his life!

The six Catholic chaplains then expressed their unanimous and vigorous opposition to any joint service, most especially to a sermon by a Jew. If the original plan were implemented, they would, all of them, refuse to participate and urge their Catholic men to abstain. At that point ten days had passed since Cuthriell had issued his invitation to me. He called me in to explain what had happened. It was at once apparent that if he persisted, the incident would become a *cause celèbre*. Though he expressed no intention to buckle under such pressure, I realized at once that I had no moral right to expose a friend, a career Navy officer, to this kind of embarrassment. Once such a scandal blotched his record, there would never be another promotion! I thanked him again and withdrew.

There was no combined religious service. After the general had concluded his remarks, each faith went to its specific corner of the cemetery to hold its own dedication. The sermon I had written for the original occasion was in fact delivered at our little Jewish service, attended in all by no more than forty or fifty men. Not one word in my manuscript was changed. Whatever may seem to reflect the sordid background just described had been written before I even knew what had happened.

Redeeming paradox: Three Protestant chaplains were so incensed at the opposition of the others that they boycotted their own service, attended mine instead. One of them borrowed my onion-skin sheets, saying he wanted to read what I had said. Unknown to me, he mimeographed several thousand copies, which he proceeded to distribute to the men of his regiment. Some of them enclosed these in letters to their families. An avalanche resulted: *Time* magazine, as well as many newspapers, published excerpts; someone inserted the entire sermon into the *Congressional Record*; several literary and oratorical anthologies included it; Robert St. John read it on his regular radio program not only then, but for many years after the war regularly on Memorial Day. I learned much later that Frederick March had read it in full over CBS, that NBC had recorded it in Hawaii, that the army had released it for short-wave broadcast to American troops throughout the world. My original manuscript has been deposited, by invitation, in the American Jewish Archives. I have often wondered whether anyone would ever have heard of my Iwo sermon had it not been for the bigoted attempt to ban it.

Was this just an aberration? The glaring exception that illumines the rule? I wish it were. Easter Sunday fell on our first weekend sailing back from Iwo to Hawaii. We had been scheduled, incidentally, to go to Guam after finishing the Iwo operation, there to be held in reserve for the impending attack on Okinawa. After five weeks on the island of black sand and volcanic ash, there were not enough of us left intact to serve in reserve for a cotillion. So we were directed back to our original camp for rehabilitation and additional training. Easter morning I stood on the fantail during Catholic Mass. In part perhaps out of curiosity; in part because, after Iwo I felt an irresistible need to share companionship and religious reinforcement with others. There, to my astonishment and chagrin, I heard the ship's Catholic chaplain, preaching on the theme of Resurrection, repeat four or five times as a litany: "Remember, men, it was the Jews who crucified our Lord! Remember . . . remember . . . remember . . . "

We had just surmounted five weeks of unutterable hell. Some of us had tried to serve men of all faiths and of no faith, without making denomination a prerequisite for fellowship. Protestants, Catholics, and Jews had lived together, fought together, bled together, died together, and now lay buried together. But we, the lucky living remnant, couldn't pray together! And we had to be reminded, presumably mandated by faith, of history's nastiest calumny! My chief consolation—then and still now—was that another Jew besides myself could not have dedicated the cemetery and would have been scurrilously assaulted by the very men who professed to teach in his name.

11
Love

Your old men shall dream dreams,
And your young men shall see visions.

Visions and dreams. Without them, no one of us could have endured Iwo. Dreams of loved ones and home. Of embraces and kisses. Of soft beds and clean sheets. Visions of a different, more decent kind of world. If this nightmare were only a violent parenthesis, if life were to resume afterward at the same level of corruption and contempt, our bloody sacrifice would be no less senseless and degenerate than that of primitive peoples who immolated their children to Moloch.

So, on 26 March 1945, standing in a quiet corner of the Fifth Marine Division Cemetery, my heart ineffably saddened at the price that had been paid and how little some of my colleagues had learned from it, I dreamed:

"This is perhaps the grimmest, and surely the holiest task we have faced since D-Day. Here before us lie the bodies of comrades and friends. Men who until yesterday or last week laughed with us, joked with us, trained with us. Men who were on the same ships with us, and went over the sides with us as we prepared to hit the beaches of this island. Men who fought with us and feared with us.

"Somewhere in this plot of ground there may lie the man who could have discovered the cure for cancer. Under one of these Christian crosses, or beneath a Jewish Star of David, there may rest now a man who was destined to be a great prophet . . . to find the way, perhaps, for all to live in plenty, with poverty and hardship for none. Now they lie here silently in this sacred soil, and we gather to consecrate this earth in their memory.

"It is not easy to do so. Some of us have buried our closest friends here. We saw these men killed before our very eyes. Any one of us might have died in their places. Indeed, some of us are alive and breathing at this very moment only because men who lie here beneath us had the courage and strength to give their lives for ours. To speak in memory of such men as these is not easy. Of them, too, can it be said with utter truth: 'The world will little note nor long remember what we say here. It can never forget what they did here.'

"No, our poor power of speech can add nothing to what these men and the other dead of our division who are not here have already done. All that we can even hope to do is follow their example. To show the same selfless courage in peace that they did in war. To swear that, by the grace of God and the stubborn strength and power of human will, their sons and ours shall never suffer these pains again. These men have done their job well. They have paid the ghastly price of freedom. If that freedom be once again lost, as it was after the last war, the unforgivable blame will be ours, not theirs. So it is we, the living, who are here to be dedicated and consecrated.

"We dedicate ourselves, first, to live together in peace the way they fought and are buried here in war. Here lie men who loved America because their ancestors generations ago helped in her founding, and other men who loved her with equal passion because they themselves or their own fathers escaped from oppression to her blessed shores. Here lie officers and men, Negroes and whites, rich men and poor . . . together. Here are Protestants,

135

Catholics, and Jews . . . together. Here no man prefers another because of his faith or despises him because of his color. Here there are no quotas of how many from each group are admitted or allowed. Among these men there is no discrimination. No prejudice. No hatred. Theirs is the highest and purest democracy.

"Any man among us, the living, who fails to understand that will thereby betray those who lie here dead. Whoever of us lifts his hand in hate against a brother, or thinks himself superior to those who happen to be in the minority, makes of this ceremony and of the bloody sacrifice it commemorates, an empty, hollow mockery. To this, then, as our solemn, sacred duty, do we the living now dedicate ourselves: to the right of Protestants, Catholics, and Jews, of white men and Negroes alike, to enjoy the democracy for which all of them have here paid the price.

"To one thing more do we consecrate ourselves in memory of those who sleep beneath these crosses and stars. We shall not foolishly suppose, as did the last generation of America's fighting men, that victory on the battlefield will automatically guarantee the triumph of democracy at home. This war, with all its frightful heartache and suffering, is but the beginning of our generation's struggle for democracy. When the last battle has been won, there will be those at home, as there were last time, who will want us to turn our backs in selfish isolation on the rest of organized humanity, and thus to sabotage the very peace for which we fight. We promise you who lie here: we will not do that! We will join hands with Britain, China, Russia—in peace, even as we have in war—to build the kind of world for which you died.

"When the last shot has been fired, there will still be those whose eyes are turned backward, not forward, who will be satisfied with those wide extremes of poverty and wealth in which the seeds of another war can breed. We promise you, our departed comrades: This too we will not permit. This war has been fought by the common man; its fruits of peace must be enjoyed by the comman man! We promise, by all that is sacred and holy, that your sons—the sons of miners and millers, the sons of farmers and workers, will inherit from your death the right to a living that is decent and secure.

"When the final cross has been placed in the last cemetery, once again there will be those to whom profit is more important than peace, who will insist with the voice of sweet reasonableness and appeasement that it is better to trade with the enemies of mankind than, by crushing them, to lose their profit. To you who sleep here silently, we give our promise: We will not listen! We will not forget that some of you were burnt with oil that came from American wells, that many of you were killed by shells fashioned from American steel. We promise that when once again men seek profit at your expense, we shall remember how you looked when we placed you reverently, lovingly, in the ground.

"Thus do we memorialize those who, having ceased living with us, now live within us. Thus do we consecrate ourselves, the living, to carry on the struggle they began. Too much blood has gone into this soil for us to let it lie barren. Too much pain and heartache have fertilized the earth on which we stand. We here solemnly swear: this shall not be in vain! Out of this, and from the suffering and sorrow of those who mourn this, will come—we promise—the birth of a new freedom for the sons of men everywhere. Amen."

How easy it would be—in rereading these words more than a generation after they were first spoken—to succumb to bleak despair. So many promises and pledges! So much firm determination to promote justice, to rectify wrongs! Where has it all gone?

. . . their sons and ours shall never suffer these pains again. But they already have. In Korea, in Cambodia, in Vietnam they have suffered these pains. And ominous signs persist that the victims and the pains may yet become greater and worse.

. . . we the living now dedicate ourselves to the right of Protestants, Catholics and Jews, of white men and Negroes alike, to enjoy the democracy for which all of them have here paid the price. Where is that right? Neo-Nazis and Klansmen run for public office, sometimes even succeed. Blacks still live in squalid slums, suffer excessive unemployment, receive inferior education. In 1984 over 80 percent of full-time undergraduate students at historically black colleges needed student loans; 42 percent of them were from families with incomes below the government poverty line.[1]

. . . We will join hands with Britain, China, Russia—in peace, even as we have in war—to build the kind of world for which you died. Yes, we have remained joined with a pitifully weakened, largely ineffectual Britain, and with China, but mostly as a weapon against Russia. When we were dramatically ahead of Russia in the race for nuclear supremacy, we squandered priceless opportunities to establish arms control. Since then, every frightful new advance in that deadly race has emanated from us.

. . . your sons . . . will inherit from your death the right to a living which is decent and secure. In the most prosperous nation history has ever known, millions of unemployed mock that solemn promise. In 1982 there were 1.6 million children in New York City. Professor Emanuel Tobier of New York University reported to New York's Community Service Society that the proportion of them living below the government's official poverty line "had probably moved

well over the 40 percent mark."[2]

. . . when once again men seek profit at your expense, we shall remember how you looked when we placed you reverently, lovingly, in the ground. The National Semiconductor Corporation pleaded guilty in 1984 to fraud against the government by knowingly selling defective computer chips to the Defense Department between 1978 and 1981. These chips were installed in fighter planes, bombers, and tanks. When, in consequence of NSC's admission of guilt, Washington disqualified the firm from bidding on new defense contracts, the corporation filed suit against the government![3]

. . . Out of this, and from the suffering and sorrow of those who mourn this, will come—we promise—the birth of a new freedom for the sons of men everywhere. For those who live in the Soviet Bloc? In the emerging new nations of Africa, where more often than not political independence has meant no more than a change of cast among the oppressors? In the nations of Latin America, where the leaders of corporation and church so often conspire to keep the people enslaved? In the Arab world, where potentates glutted with oil wealth assume a larger and larger share of control over world economy, with little or no improvement for the masses of their peoples?

Indeed, it is easy—almost irresistibly so—to succumb to bleak despair. Is there, then, no hope? Has there been no progress? Some, to be sure. Though difficult to measure statistically, I believe that larger numbers of individuals and organizations today than in 1945 are alert to the menace that hangs so ominously over our heads. There is greater awareness that, in order to survive, democracy must be more widely introduced into the marketplace than it has thus far been.

Far more important than the notoriety achieved by my Iwo sermon was the solace it apparently brought to some who needed it most. I still have a few of their letters. A grieving woman in California wrote:

> I have just finished reading over and over your address as a memorial to Marines who gave their lives on Iwo Jima. It was beautiful in (the) sense that it is a challenge to those alive. . . .
>
> It meant a great deal to me and I shall reread it many times more—for as you spoke, you were speaking of one very dear to me. My brother Bob gave his life on March 10 on Iwo. Because of that white cross to mark his grave, a gold star hangs in the window at home. His room holds his skis, his fishing rods, his guns. His pictures of our birds and outdoor life hang upon the walls just as he placed them there.
>
> Bob will never live in that room again, but the memories will always be there. He was such a swell brother. It's hard to read the tragic words "killed in action" and realize that he will never return to those he loved and who loved him. . . .
>
> Bob has gone to his Maker. . . . He never did a bad or mean act in all his 19 years. If you could give me any information about Bob's death and burial, I would appreciate it so very much. I want to know if he was killed instantly or died of wounds—anything you can write about him. . . .
>
> You probably have received many letters such as mine, all grasping for direct information. Every little bit means so much.

From a heart-broken mother in Florida:

> In a recent issue of *Time* excerpts from your sermon dedicating the Fifth Marine Division cemetery on Iwo Jima were given. Our son . . . sleeps there with his buddies,

"forever young" and at peace: no more suffering, no more fighting. It was his first action, I think. He was killed Feb. 20—we know no details. . . .

Will you contact men of this company, who may know how he died, asking them to write us, or to tell you, please? These boys are so young; they have not known life as [men]. Surely you spoke a great truth when you told what they might have given the world, had they been spared. Theirs is indeed "the highest and purest democracy." Here is true equality as God means it to be on earth. I cannot believe God sent this war as a punishment for our misdeeds. He neither makes nor ends wars! This is man-made misery!

I know God grieves for the "little people" of this sad earth, who always pay the awful price of war in lives and suffering—they are so helpless! I wish I might read all of your sermon—it would be like a service in honor of the boy we love so well. May I have a copy, please?

Thank you for these beliefs—when these become the creed of the earth, there will be real and lasting peace. May God guide you in teaching them.

I struggle intensely to escape the trap of pessimism toward which the facts of life often impel me. Even as, admittedly on a much simpler level, I assumed—and won— that struggle in a corner of the Iwo cemetery and on board ship that Easter Sunday morning. The temptation was strong to brood morbidly over the circumstances surrounding the sermon I gave on Iwo and the one I heard while sailing back to Hawaii. To conclude that the Christian world consisted only of enemies. Fortunately, there was evidence to the contrary.

The young lieutenant who warned me that I was being investigated, Warren Cuthriell with his willingness to jeopardize his career by practicing his preachments, the three Protestant chaplains who worshiped with my Jewish boys rather than their own co-religionists—all these were Christians, all these in one way or another stuck their necks out unnecessarily on my behalf, all these kept me from surrendering my final hope in humanity.

The publicity given my cemetery sermon infuriated the chaplains who had originally objected to my giving it. One of them, twisting the facts to support his own jaundiced view, reported me as being anti-Christian to the Senior District Chaplain, the same man who, deliberately or not, later left my personnel file where I could see it. In it I found a letter that Chaplain Dumstrey wrote to my colleague on 11 May 1945:

> Following our recent conversation, I inquired into the other side of the point in question. It seems that you are not entirely without fault, that in both word and deed you have contradicted the high standards of a true Christian gentleman and the principles of freedom of religion so dear to the hearts of American citizens, which have been at stake in the European conflict.
>
> I deeply regret that one of your calling should take the stand which it appears you have taken. It serves no good purpose, especially in the service. We are a conglomerate group, a mixture of racial, religious and national antecedents. All have their constitutional rights and privileges. As a minister of religion, you should be among the first to champion rather than to scorn them.

While still stationed in San Diego, where I had to cover a half-dozen or so installations, I was able to visit the Marine Corps Base only once a week. During the interval between two of my visits, a Jewish youngster came for counseling to Walter Mahler, Senior Chaplain at the Base. Part of the boy's problem was that he wore his Jewishness with uncomfortable awkwardness. This was the first time in his life that he had lived in a predominantly non-Jewish environment; he felt exposed to ridicule and was ashamed of being a Jew. It would have been easy—and officially acceptable—for Chaplain Mahler to have passed the buck, to arrange an appointment for the young man on my next visit.

Instead, he patiently said to the distraught Marine, "Don't let me ever catch you walking around this base ashamed of being a Jew! As a Catholic priest, I get down on my knees every morning to pray to a Jew. I hold a Jewish girl to be one of the most sacred personalities of my faith. You just walk out of this office and hold your head high; being a Jew is something to be proud of, not something to hide!" I doubt that anything I might have said as a rabbi could have restored this young man's Jewish self-respect as effectively as these words of a Catholic priest.

At the same Marine Corps Base in advance of Passover 1944, the messmen and cooks—among them Greeks, Italians, Scotch-Irish, but not a single Jew—worked for weeks, laid in supplies, studied Jewish recipes, prepared gefilte fish and matzo-ball soup, borrowed sheets for tablecloths and filled old catsup bottles with flowers—all in order that seventy Jewish men and women could sit down to a traditional *seder* dinner. On Christmas and Easter, the same thing was true in reverse: scores of Jewish men volunteered for extra duty so that Christians could celebrate their sacred days.

There were others too. Herbert Van Meter was one of them. We first met as classmates at the College of William and Mary, where the Naval Training School for Chaplains was located in the summer of 1943. A series of coincidences led to both of us being assigned on graduation to the San Diego area, then to the Fifth Marine Division. We and our wives became close friends, often having dinner together on Saturday nights during our months of training at Pendleton. When our division was shipped out over a period of weeks to Hawaii, in order that I might be present wherever the majority of our troops was at a given time, I remained in California until more than half the men had arrived in the Pacific, then was flown across to join them.

Arriving at Kamuela on Hawaii, I discovered that Herb had, on his own initiative, been conducting Friday night religious services for the Jewish men. Some of them were even calling him *Rabbi Van Meter.* Though many miles separated us after our discharge from the Navy, Herb and I kept in touch with each other thirty-two years and visited as often as we could. His untimely death in early 1982 was an intensely personal loss to me.

My experience with Carl Elder was even more dramatic. He was an Army chaplain; we first met on Iwo. Every Friday night he not only rounded up the Jewish men in his outfit for Sabbath services, he came with them and joined in our Jewish worship. One day I happened to lament in his presence that, because I had ordered all my Passover supplies to be shipped to Guam, and because our plans had changed so that we would not be on Guam at all, there was no way in the world for me to meet the holiday needs of Jewish Marines who would be in transit when Passover began. I promptly forgot this conversation.

Four or five days later, my field telephone rang. "Roland? This is Carl. Get yourself over here to my area with a jeep or truck. I have half-a-ton of Passover gear for you and the other Jewish chaplains." Carl had coopted a cargo plane, flown to Saipan, brought back *matzot,* gefilte fish, wine, and *haggadot,* the supplies that I so "dexterously" delivered, despite an uncooperative wind, to the ships of our convoy.

A few years after the war, Carl happened to be in the New York area at Passover time. He came as a guest of honor to our congregational *seder* in Rockville Centre, where I told the story of his helpfulness and the congregation stood to applaud him.

Antidotes to prejudice and hate were abundant among the enlisted men as well as officers and chaplains. The most memorable combat photograph I saw was one snapped by a Jewish corporal who happened, quite by coincidence, to come across two Marines—a Protestant and a Catholic—kneeling in prayer at the grave of a Jewish friend. One morning two Christian boys, observing the chaplain's insignia on my combat fatigues, asked me to pray with them over the grave of a Jewish buddy.

Among the names of Jewish Marines inscribed on my memory indelibly was that of Sid Randall, a youngster from Boston. He was tall, solid, strong. A day or so before we turned Iwo over to army occupation troops, I came across Sid in the cemetery, crying copiously over the grave of a Christian friend. The next time I saw him was seven years later when, after assuming rabbinic leadership of Temple Israel of Boston, I found Sid among my new congregants. I see him frequently, have confirmed and married his daughters. We seldom talk about our shared combat experience; Sid still finds it difficult to ventilate his pain.

An extraordinary thing happened just a few days before our departure from the island. Each grave was marked by a white wooden cross or star. The men discovered somehow that the sandstone on the north end of Iwo could be smoothed and carved. They began spontaneously to make headstones for the graves of friends. When I walked through our cemetery the last evening we were on Iwo, there must have been three to four hundred such stones, each carved by a man who had already expended his last ounce of strength in combat but could not leave without a final tribute to someone he loved. No one bothered to inquire whether the faith of the carver matched that of the deceased.

So it is. In war and peace, in politics and economics, here at home and abroad—so it is. Good people and bad. Selfish individuals and altruists. Those who plan hopefully for the future and those who greedily hug the past. We must resist despair, lest our predictions of doom become self-fulfilling prophecies. The ancient rabbis put it very well: Act at each moment as if all humanity is exactly balanced between good and evil, so that what you do next will determine the outcome.

Notes

1. *New York Times*, 1 April 1987.
2. Reported by Anthony Lewis in the *New York Times*, 4 April 1985.
3. Reported by Marshall L. Raines Associate Professor of Advertising, San Jose State University, in the *New York Times*, 31 July 1984.

12
Zion

At age fourteen I was nearly thrown out of the confirmation class at Cleveland's Euclid Avenue Temple. My grades were excellent; I had been given an award for attendance; no teacher had ever complained about my behavior. Why, then, the threat of expulsion? Because then, as now, I was given to vehement argumentation. Alone among my fellow-students, I disputed Rabbi Louis Wolsey's views on Zionism. I don't know whether he was aware of the fact that my father was probably the only pronounced Zionist in a congregation which then numbered some four or five hundred families, but he certainly didn't expect one of his ninth-grade students to debate him in class.

On earlier pages I have already mentioned the profound impression that Dad's love of Palestine and his Zionist fervor made on me in my childhood. No account of my career and its priorities would be adequate without pursuing in some detail my work on behalf of a Jewish State.

In fairness to Rabbi Wolsey, his attitude was typical of most Reform rabbis at that time. He argued against Zionism on two grounds: (1) Palestine wasn't big enough to hold all the world's Jews; (2) we Jews had a mission to teach ethics to the world and for the fulfillment of that mission were destined to live scattered among the nations, not in a homeland of our own.

My responses, then and now: (1) the Zionist ideal does

not demand that every Jew in the world make Israel his personal homeland; (2) a people scattered and despised everywhere is not likely to command the respect required for effective teaching. Far from being inconsistent with the notion that we Jews bear a mission to instruct all humanity, the establishment of a self-respecting and respect-inducing Jewish community in an autonomous Jewish State may well be a pre-condition for such a mission.

Louis Wolsey was far from the only person—Jew or non-Jew—to misconstrue the essential meaning of Zionism. The equation by the UN of Zionism with racism may be history's most shameless slander. What, then—reduced to intentional oversimplification—is the Zionist movement really about? What are its basic purposes and aims?

(1) Only the re-establishment of a Jewish State can effectively cure the virus of anti-Semitism, from which we Jews have suffered so grievously. We shall then, as a people, have an address as well as an agency in the council of nations to protect our rights wherever they may be threatened.

(2) Individual Jews whose lives are made intolerable in other lands will have a place to which they may go and in which they may live, free of persecution.

(3) The survival of Judaism and the Jewish people will be rendered more probable. During the past two millennia, the internal drive of the Jewish community to persist was constantly reinforced by the external pressures of anti-Semitism. With those pressures relaxed, with ghetto walls crumbled and entrance of Jews into the larger world facilitated, with the threat of total assimilation thereby immeasurably increased, there is grave danger that, lacking a concentrated center, Jews and their continuing heritage may cease to exist as identifiable historic entities.

(4) To survive and develop creatively, a civilization

must have a locus, a laboratory or hot-house, if you will, where it can be the primary culture of its people, where new strands and strains may be tested and refined.

Zionists insist that Judaism is not a dead fossil. If it were to disappear from the stage of history tomorrow, of course whatever it has already contributed to civilization would persist as part of the mainstream. But there would be no further Judaic infusions. Civilizations do not evolve in vacuums; they develop out of the living experience of specific peoples, in specific places and times. Each such people, like every individual, has its own unique thread to weave into the fabric of civilization, expressive of its collective nature and personality. To continue developing, to expand what it has already given, thus enriching still further the total human heritage, it must have its own place of creative development. For Jewish civilization, that place is Israel.

Ironically, not only Israel's enemies, some of its staunchest friends also misconstrue the full dimension of Zionism. Take my good friend Ben Halpern, for example. One of the ideological leaders of American Zionism, he recently wrote: "Reduced to its simplest terms, Zionism aims to make a normal—that is, an ordinary—nation of the Jewish people." Nonsense! This reduces Zionism not to its simplest terms but to a caricature. We Jews have never been an ordinary people; this has been a seed of our problem in history. The minute that Israel, God forbid, becomes ordinary or normal, it will cease being a *Jewish* state.

Theodore Herzl, founder of modern Zionism, knew this. He anticipated a state that would be "an outpost of civilization against barbarism." He said that Zionism must mean a revival of Judaism before it could produce the revival of a Jewish State. A. D. Gordon, seminal shaper of

149

Labor Zionism, knew this too. He reminded his contemporaries: "We Jews were the first to teach the world that human beings are created in the image of God. The purpose of a Jewish State," he added, "must be to refashion the entire Jewish people in a divine image."

David Ben Gurion, one of Israel's architects and its first Prime Minister, also understood the full meaning of Zionism. He wrote: "The State of Israel will be judged not by its riches or military power, nor by its technical skills, but by its moral worth and human values. . . . [M]erely to be like all other peoples is not enough."

Herzl knew . . . Gordon knew . . . Ben Gurion knew. Unfortunately, too many people today do not know. They confuse means with ends. They fail to realize that the Jewish state—imperative and indispensable though it surely be—is still only a means. Its end is the liberation and continued creativity of the whole Jewish people—the *whole* Jewish people, with those who live most intensely Jewish lives in Israel providing a paradigm for those who remain in other countries. If the state as such ever becomes the ultimate end of Zionism, we shall have prostituted the meaning of Jewish nationalism. We shall then have fashioned another Molten Calf.

Is Israel the product of and governed by Jewish paranoia? The question reminds me of Saul Bellow's quip: "I may be paranoid, but that doesn't stop people from plotting against me." Paranoia is a diseased reaction to danger that either doesn't exist or has been exaggerated far beyond reality. There is, alas, nothing in the least imaginary about the enmity that has been directed against us Jews. We have been history's most ubiquitous scapegoat. Both Christianity and Islam have branded us as cursed by God. Every blight of nature—earthquake, plague, flood, all of them—has been blamed on us. Our history in medieval times was traumatically punctuated by repeated inquisition and expulsion.

During the worst depth of the depravity called Holocaust, there were ships to transport almost 400,000 prisoners of war to camps in the United States, but none to save Jews. There were RAF Mosquitoes and Spitfires to free members of the French Resistance from an Amiens prison but none to bomb concentration camps. The leaders of Britain and the United States were available to consult with every conceivable ally, but Franklin Roosevelt deliberately evaded four hundred rabbis who wanted to meet with him and Winston Churchill refused to see Chaim Weizmann, president of the World Zionist Organization. The UN embraces every liberation movement on earth, even those that would liberate only a new group of dictators to tyrannize their people, but condemns the liberation movement of the Jewish people as racism.

Paranoia? Not by the wildest stretch of the most perverted imagination! The danger that alerts Jews is as real as cancer. The prejudice aimed against Jews is the most pervasively ferocious in history. There would be something truly psychotic about any people who failed to recognize and resist such venom.

Two personal experiences will shed more light on this alleged Jewish paranoia than many pages of additional exposition.

The first of my many visits to *Yad Vashem*, the Holocaust Memorial outside Jerusalem, took place in 1964. We were with our dearest friends, Rabbi and Mrs. Jacob Rudin, and an Israeli guide who had miraculously survived seven concentration camps. The five of us stood silently in the Tent of Remembrance, almost morbidly mesmerized by the stark, unfinished concrete ceiling and walls, the flickering Eternal Flame, the six million tiny tiles on the floor spelling

151

out in Roman and Hebrew letters the infamous names of the camps, covering in each case human ashes removed from that place.

We cried without inhibition or shame. No word was spoken, until our guide, almost as if whispering to himself, quietly murmured, "I like to think my mother's ashes are here; it makes me feel better."

From the Tent itself, we proceeded to the adjoining Holocaust Museum. It takes a stout heart and a strong stomach to view the photographs and remnants gathered there without suffering haunting nightmares. Who can ever forget the tiny torn shoe, retrieved from one of the camps, now enshrined in glass to symbolize the million and a half innocent little children who were among the six million Jewish victims of Hitler's hosts?

Our guide stopped us at the entrance to the museum. He described in considerable detail what we would see there, then apologized: "Please forgive me for not entering with you. It's more than I can bear. Take all the time you want and try to remember any questions you may have. I'll be waiting for you at the exit and will try to answer your questions there."

A more recent experience is equally poignant. In 1981 the Jewish Agency for Israel held a three-day conference at Caesarea. After an opening keynote address, we were divided into smaller working groups, each consisting in equal proportion of Israeli and Diaspora Jews. By a stroke of genius, the conference planners had decreed that in these more intimate sessions we were to commence by having each person briefly offer his or her Zionist autobiography, that is to say, how he or she had become actively involved in work for Israel. I shall never, *never* forget the story told by one of my Israeli colleagues on the Agency Board of Governors. He and I have voted on opposite sides of just about every substantive issue that has come before us—on West Bank settlements, on attempting to negotiate with the Arab nations, on Israel's defense needs and policies. He is aggressively militant on all these, I more inclined to seek compromise. Let me relate his account, so far as memory will permit, in his own words:

> My older sister and I are the only members of our family to escape the Warsaw Ghetto. She was 12 years old at the time. Even after the war was over, we had to flee from the Polish partisans, who hated and harassed Jews no less than the Nazis.
>
> The two of us wandered in the woods together for almost a year. I was convinced we were the only Jews left in the world. We ate whatever we could find growing or could steal from a farm. Many times I wanted to give up. My sister wouldn't allow it. Whenever I weakened and was ready to surrender, she used a magic word to revive me. The magic word was *Palestine*. I never quite knew where or what Palestine was, but my sister kept telling me it was a place where we would join other Jews, where we would have a country at last of our own, where no one could force us to keep running away. Now we are in that home.

I shall no doubt continue to disagree with this man at future meetings and to vote against his views. But I cannot blame or condemn him. If I came from where he did, if I had experienced what he has and stood where he is now, perhaps I would feel the same way.

This is not paranoia. This is harsh, grim, gruesome reality. Thank God, it's only half the story. The approach to Yad Vashem is a graceful promenade of trees, each planted in honor or memory of a Gentile who rescued numbers of Jews from the Holocaust. Documentation for each of these heroes is deposited in the adjoining archives. On my second visit to Yad Vashem in 1970, our guide detained us after the bus had stopped and the door had been opened. "Before you leave the bus," he said, "I want to call your attention to these trees." He then proceeded to explain their significance and added:

All this will mean more to you if I first tell you the story of one Italian Catholic. When Mussolini started to ape the anti-Semitism of Hitler, this man hid a large group of Jews in his cellar. Obviously, he risked his life in doing so. After the Germans had actually invaded Italy, it was no longer possible to keep his Jews at home, so, a few at a time under cover of night, he led them to an isolated spot in the forest. Somehow he succeeded in evading Nazi surveillance to bring them food several times a week and to keep them alive to the end of the war. Of the 50-odd Jewish men and women whom he saved, 46 came to Israel.

Then a pause, a stifled sob, and—

One of them is my wife!

It is easy to trace historically the millennial role of Zionism in Jewish life. It is quite another and more vivid experience to feel the connection in the very marrow of one's bones.

I never walk through the excavations at Caesarea without wondering whether, unknowingly and inadvertently, I may have stepped on the very spot where Rabbi Akiva was burned at the stake by the Romans in the second century. Or, in the Judean Hills, has my foot ever trod exactly where Amos stood, where Isaiah and Jeremiah excoriated their kings and passionately pleaded for justice, where Jesus pronounced his Sermon on the Mount? In reverently examining tombstones on the Mount of Olives, most sacred Jewish cemetery of all ages, have I walked over the place where my sixteenth-century rabbinic ancestor, Rabbi Isaiah Horowitz, may have been buried? To ask such questions is to relate myself in the deepest possible dimension to all my people's aspiration and hope from the begining of Jewish time.

Nowhere is this truer than at the Western Wall, the only remaining remnant of the ancient Temple. On the first two of my twenty-one visits to Israel, I was unable to approach or even see the Wall; no Jew was allowed there by the Jordanians who, by dint of military conquest, controlled East Jerusalem until after the war of 1967. Commencing with my visit of 1970, I have never gone to Jerusalem without praying at the Wall, usually several times, nearly always within an hour or so of my arrival.

My favorite time there is at night, when there are few people, no distractions or noises. When soft floodlights bathe the stones in gold and beige, when the vines pushing so persistently between the stones seem to whisper gently into one's ear. There, more than anywhere else on earth, I am alone with my God.

I am not a mystic. In fact, truth be told, unbridled mysticism frightens me. The one place in the world where I could imagine myself perhaps becoming a mystic is Israel, especially Jerusalem, most especially at the Wall. Quite often my father reminded me of the midrashic assertion that *aveerah d'eretz Yisra-ayl machkeemah*—the air of the Land of Israel makes one wise. I do not know whether that ancient assertion is true or not, but I am certain there is something about the ambience and atmosphere of this sacred land that makes it an ideal meeting place for the human and the divine. Small wonder that Judaism, Christianity, and Islam were all conceived in this womb!

I always kiss the Wall three times before caressing its cold stones—once for myself, once each for my grandfather

155

and father who revered it vicariously, who first inspired my fascination for it, but who were never privileged to see or touch it. When I have finished praying, I study the faces and demeanor of others standing nearby—Israelis and visitors, civilians and soldiers, those who believe and those who usually scoff, among the former every degree from the most devoutly Orthodox to the most rationalistically Reform. The Wall captivates every Jew, transforms each of us into something different from what he normally is or feels. For centuries Jews have stuffed little pieces of paper bearing their petitions into the crevices of the Wall, believing that in some mysterious way such messages merit God's very special attention. What heartache and hope these bits of paper bear, what worry and grief, what anxiety and guilt! Am I being cynical in wondering how many of them express gratitude?

One sunny morning I turned from my own devotions at the Wall to witness three young men, apparently brothers. The two who appeared to be in their late teens or early twenties were in uniform. The youngest, about twelve or thirteen, was crying uncontrollably; the others embraced him lovingly, dried his tears, whispered to him words of reassurance and strength. What was it they shared in common? The serious illness or death of mother or father? The imminent departure of the older ones for military duty? The news that someone dear to them had been killed in combat? I'll never know. But this I do know: if there is one place on earth where a Jew feels a blessed fusion of his spirit with God's, where he can touch the hem of his people's history, that place is the Wall.

13

Testament

The setting was incomparably magnificent. Five hundred Americans—Reform rabbis and their wives—were gathered in the outdoor amphitheatre of the Hebrew University on Mount Scopus. They looked out, over and beyond the stage on which a few of us sat, into the surrounding desert and hills. They saw a bright, azure sky . . . the hazy, mauve-tinted Hills of Judea . . . off in the distance the metallic surface of the Dead Sea . . . a lone Arab shepherd prodding his reluctant sheep slowly across the foreground valley.

And I? I was incredibly lucky to be President at that very time of the Central Conference of American Rabbis, thus to preside, in March of 1970, over the first modern convention of rabbis ever held in Jerusalem. After a special liturgy prepared for the occasion had been concluded, I stood at the lectern alone. Yet I was not alone; almost palpably I could feel the presence of others. David was there and Solomon, ancient kings who first conquered Jerusalem, then made it the spiritual capital of our faith. Josephus was at my side, the militarist-historian who wrote nineteen centuries ago that from this very mountain the Romans launched their final attack on our Temple. The messengers of the Sanhedrin were with me, those who on this very hill each month lit the first in a series of beacon lights signalling to Jews everywhere that the new moon had been seen, another month had commenced.

In my Presidential Address, I touched on two themes: First, the inextricable interweaving of religion and nationality in the fabric of Judaism, a relationship that makes the Jewish people unique and that sometimes makes it difficult even for us Jews to define ourselves.

I said:

> Anyone who distorts the tradition to make it appear as only religion or only nationalism will have concocted an aberrant monstrosity which will not be authentic Judaism. The first generations of Reform Jews made the mistake of amputating the ethnic and national from our heritage. Some Israelis assume the opposite risk of perceiving Judaism to be only a nationalism like all other nationalisms. We must remember that without either religion or nationalism there is no historically valid Judaism.

I then proceeded to the even more difficult task of defining who or what is a religious Jew, starting with the premise that neither American nor Israeli Jews have come close yet to a satisfactory understanding. "Both perspectives partake of partial truth; neither is entirely true." Our mistake has been to equate Jewish religion with synagogue worship, theirs to assume that religion is limited to outworn symbols and forms. By way of illustrating the latter:

> Moshe Dayan is not a [religious person]. His interview with Jacques Boetsch, a French journalist, was reprinted last June by the *New York Times Magazine* . . . Dayan confessed categorically: "I am not religious." Then, in two astonishing sentences, he added: "I know my history, and I want my children to be raised in this history. I want them to have a high opinion of it—not as concerns the religion, but as it concerns the philosophy of Judaism—justice, mercy, the equality of people and the idea that God made man in His own image." So this is what it means for a good

Jew to be non-religious: the affirmation that God made man in His own image!

The closest I could come to answering my own question was the following:

> More than any other people on earth, we Jews have refused to settle for the status of cosmic orphans. We have needed to know how we belong, not only on this planet, but among all the planets and suns and galaxies. We have insisted on exploring our relationship with the larger universe both physically and spiritually. Our faith can be defined as spiritual ecology. Any Jew who believes that ultimate reality is spiritual as well as physical, and that he himself is intimately related to that ultimate reality is a religious Jew, whether or not he uses the exact theological vocabulary of the past.

Everything I had said or done about Zionism prior to 1977 culminated in my election as Founding President of ARZA (pronounced ARTSA), the Association of Reform Zionists of America. With a plethora of Zionist organizations already existing, why did we Reform Jews deem it necessary to initiate a new one of our own? For several reasons. First and foremost, to encourage the development of religious options for our fellow-Jews in Israel. A strange anomaly is involved here. The Orthodox religious parties in Israel, constituting no more than 10 to 12 percent of the population, exert highly disproportionate political influence as well as a near-monopoly over the nation's religious life.

This strange distortion results from two factors, one historic, the other political. From the time of Turkish hegemony over what was then Palestine, and extending into the British mandatory period, all religious matters—Christian, Moslem, Jewish—were placed exclusively in the

Addressing children of Temple Israel Religious School when they honored him on his retirement, June 5, 1977.

hands of ecclesiastical leaders. Since at that time the only rabbis in the country were Orthodox, there was no question as to the locus of Jewish religious authority. The state of Israel at its inception was beset with so many more immediately urgent problems that this system was continued without interruption.

Politically, there has never been a single party in Israel strong enough to achieve majority support by itself. As a result, the party winning a plurality has always had to woo smaller factions in order to form a ruling coalition. The several religious parties, especially when combining their strength, have thus far proved themselves to be the most eligible and available partners. In return for their support on other issues, they have demanded and received exclusive control over religious matters. If politics makes strange bedfellows, politics and religion together make even more puzzling companions.

This helps us understand Moshe Dayan's peculiar ideas of religion. Like his fellow-Israelis, until very recently he had only two options: either to be strictly Orthodox, punctiliously observing all the minutiae of religious ritual as they were practiced in the sixteenth century, or to be a total secularist. The Orthodox Establishment would allow no alternatives, no way of being a Jewish religionist in modern terms. In an earlier chapter, I described the rigid intransigency of many Orthodox leaders today in the United States. Like Lot's wife, they gaze only backward. Like Lot's wife, they risk turning themselves and their Judaism into a pillar of salt. This is especially true in Israel.

It was largely to correct this enforced but unacceptable uniformity that ARZA was organized. As a constituent of the World Zionist Organization—the primary deliberative body representing the Jews of Israel and those of the Diaspora together vis-à-vis the Jewish State, the closest thing

161

there is to an international Jewish parliament—we can exert our influence toward encouraging the development of non-Orthodox religious Judaism in Israel. Plainly and simply, we want Israelis to have the choice already available to Jews in all other countries of selecting from among alternative interpretations of Jewish religion.

One of our first discoveries was a tremendous restlessness on this issue among the Israelis themselves. Especially in the kibbutzim, where the most idealistic of all Israelis have created and sustain a type of voluntary collective settlement unique to Israel. In the beginning, national aspiration and hope—the establishment, development, and defense of their State—was the highest loyalty these *kibbutznikim* thought they needed. More and more of them are now commencing to realize that an even higher loyalty is required, that cosmic address to which I referred in earlier paragraphs.

By virtue of my position in the leadership of ARZA, I sat for seven years also on the Executive of the World Zionist Organization. At one of our meetings in Israel, Raanan Weitz made a spontaneous statement I shall never forget. Let me explain first that Weitz is one of the world's leading experts on rural resettlement; as a result of his phenomenally successful work in Israel, he has been invited to advise a dozen or more other governments. The statement I made at the meeting in question, emphasizing the religious component in Judaism and Zionism, was to be expected; after all, I am a rabbi and a religious Zionist. Coming from one who had always identified himself as a secularist, however, Raanan's response was astonishing:

> My grandfather and father would turn in their graves if they could hear what I am about to say. They were both socialists, convinced that socialism and religion are irrecon-

Addressing Reform Zionist meeting in Jerusalem, February 1980.

cilable. I began my career with the same conviction. But I have come to realize that there is no such thing as secular Judaism, and there can be no Jewish survival without religion.

It would be unforgivably dishonest and inaccurate to pretend that anything like a majority of Israelis agree with Weitz. An impressively growing number, however, have begun to move in his direction. The late Yigal Allon was one of them. Successively Labor Minister, Foreign Minister, and Deputy Prime Minister in several Israel governments, Yigal and I had collaborated on grounds both of common ideology and close personal friendship. Eight days before his death in 1979, he and I were the principal speakers at an ARZA sponsored meeting in Jerusalem; our theme: the need of Reform Judaism and Zionism for each other.

This is the previously untapped reservoir, the almost limitless source of creative strength, which ARZA would energize. Neither Reform nor Conservative Judaism as we know them in the United States can be imported into Israel. Both are movements indigenous to our circumstances and needs on this continent. Israelis will have to develop their own varieties of non-Orthodox Judaism, responsive to *their* circumstances and *their* needs. Our aim is to encourage them by example, and to help them release the restrictions that have thus far shackled them.

Increasing the *quantity* of Jewish religious interpretations in Israel is only part of our purpose; of even greater importance, we are determined to improve the *quality* of religion. In concentrating exclusively (and compulsively) on matters of ritual, Orthodox extremists in Israel risk ignoring the ethical imperatives of Judaism.

Am I suspect in making this charge because I am a

Reform rabbi? Then let me call to the witness stand a colleague whose Orthodox credentials are impeccable, my cherished friend of many years, Rabbi Emanuel Rackman, past-President of the (Orthodox) Rabbinical Council of America, currently Chancellor of Bar Ilan University in Israel: "Many of us, Orthodox rabbis in Israel and elsewhere, are giving Jewish law a bad image. We are making it appear that *halachah* (Jewish law) is concerned only with ritual. We become exercised over violations of the sanctity of the Sabbath and remain silent with regard to the unconscionable rates of interest prevailing in the Jewish State, despite biblical and talmudic prohibitions against them."

We in ARZA are determined that in Israel, as here in the United States, Judaism must challenge us to confront compelling moral issues. On the maldistribution of wealth, on discrimination and slums, on ethics in government and business, on sexism and abortion—on these and all similar issues involving equity and justice, we insist that the voice of religion be heard. If not, our emphasis on ritual degenerates into empty pretense.

The kind of state Israel will be in the twenty-first century hinges on our success. For the same individuals and groups whose attitudes on religion are so narrowly restricted view the larger social scene with the same muddled myopia. And they will, by default if not sharply challenged, shape Israel's society into another ingrown, parochial, Levantine mold. There are signs of this already. The religio-political leaders of the Establishment have already forced their government to retrench on autopsy and abortion; they have denounced the peace treaty with Egypt and resist any kind of compromise regarding the West Bank; they oppose enlightened sex education as well as equality for women. They do not embrace or even accept the more liberal views to be found within traditional Orthodoxy itself. No one has a right to infringe on their way of teaching and practicing Judaism. By the same token, however, neither do they have a right to force their obstructionist vision on the entire state. In this respect ARZA is pushing for more than just theological alternatives as such. We aim to employ the thrust of liberal religion to the end that a modern society may prevail.

We have allies among the Israelis, so far only a few—in the near future, we hope, many more. After the election of June 1981—returning Menachem Begin to power by so tenuous a margin, leaving him so precariously dependent upon wooing the most benighted of Orthodox extremists—Meir Merhav, a Jerusalem journalist, in speculating on what four more years of a reactionary administration might make of Israeli society, used such phrases as "a second Rhodesia," "a medieval theocracy," and "a replica of a Polish or Moroccan ghetto."

When Orthodox fanatics blocked extremely important archaeological excavations because ancient graves might thereby be disturbed, one of the country's leading daily papers, *Haaretz*, editorialized: "The question before us is not whether the historical City of David will be uncovered to allow us the opportunity to learn something about life in that period. The main question is what our life-style will be in the present. Will we live as free people in spirit, mind and action, or will we be ruled by the darkness of the Middle Ages at the end of the 20th century?"

We in ARZA also believe that the noblest insights of Jewish religious tradition must be brought to bear on the nagging problem of relations with the Arabs. True, in the long light of history, the Arabs have been the aggressors and Israel the aggrieved. True, nothing can be surrendered that would further jeopardize Israel's security. Yet the sur-

166

rounding Arab nations can be waved away by neither a magic wand nor a chauvinistic firebrand. The voice of our ancestors is challengingly clear: "You shall not oppress the stranger, for you were strangers in the land of Egypt." "To me, O Israelites, you are just like the Ethiopians. True, I brought Israel up from Egypt, but also the Philistines from Caphtor and the Arameans from Kir." These words were proclaimed at times of no less danger to ancient Israel than is the present moment for modern Israel. We believe they still express the will of God.

So do some Israelis themselves. In June of 1980, my wife and I were privileged to participate in one of the most unusual meetings of our lives. Under the auspices of the World Union for Progressive Judaism and its rabbis in Israel, a summer camp session had been planned for Jewish and Arab adolescents. Rabbi Richard Hirsch, Executive Director of the World Union, invited us to join him at an all-day orientation session for prospective counselors. Like the youngsters who would arrive in a few days, these counselors were evenly divided between Jews and Arabs; most of them were social workers or teachers.

We shared with them the experience of getting acquainted with each other, of exploring their hopes not only for the impending camp term but for Jewish-Arab relations in general. One extremely bright, vivacious girl related how, at an earlier encounter with a different cast, she had voiced her aspirations for inter-group relations without identifying her own ethnic origins and how one of the Arabs present wasn't even aware of the fact that she herself is Arab until she informed him so at the end. Since 1980 these exciting camp sessions have been repeated each summer.

Incidentally—correction: far from incidentally—the actual camp session, involving approximately forty Arab and forty Jewish teenagers, exceeded even our most optimistic expectations that hot day at Hadassim. We dared to dream; they turned our dream into reality.

Another American participant at our counselors' meeting was my colleague, Bruce Cohen. Several years ago he left the congregational pulpit to found and direct Interns for Peace, an organization that trains Jews and Arabs to work together in villages of both ethnic compositions. Thus far these are lonely voices in the Middle East, even lonelier and fewer among the Arabs than with us. But history has been made by small groups of visionaries, has it not? And ARZA is determined to increase the number and volume of those who feel compelled by religious faith to work for the peace we are positive God wants.

There is a mood of disappointment, even of disillusionment, among some Zionists today. Perhaps this is a natural and inevitable reaction from the euphoria induced by Israel's earliest decades. Perhaps we expected too much, over-idealized reality, confused the first Jewish State in two thousand years with the messiah. Perhaps by expecting or assuming perfection, we rendered ourselves incapable of accepting anything less. For nearly two thousand years, we Jews carried our homeland in our hearts. It could therefore be a perfect place, without blemish or flaw, not vulnerable to the stresses and faults of a real state in a real world. In a major address to my colleagues at the 1981 convention of the Central Conference of American Rabbis in Jerusalem, I put it this way:

> You and I must never—I repeat, *never* take this State for granted. We dare not allow ourselves to become blasé about it. . . . This State, with all its deficiencies and defects, is the closest thing to a miracle any of us has ever known. Had it only rescued and resuscitated 3 million of our

brothers and sisters from the pit of hell, *dayaynu* [it would have been enough for us]. Had it only established an island of democracy in a turbulent sea of despotic dictatorships, *dayaynu*. Had it only created and sustained academies, universities, medical schools, *yeshivot*, orchestras—all among the finest on earth, *dayaynu*.

. . . how much more astonishing, then—doubly, yea triply astonishing—that Israel has accomplished all this while also enhancing the dignity and life of every Jew in the world!

In speaking thus, I articulated not only my own view but that of ARZA as well. While criticizing that which needs correction in Israel, we shall also remind ourselves and the world of those respects in which Israel remains creatively unique. The spirit of visionary excitement that brought this new nation to birth still lives.

When I am tempted by despair and doubt, I think of my first visit to Israel in 1958. Our guide, pointing to undulating waves of sand dunes on the shore, excitedly described how on that very spot Israel would build a major port and industrial city to be called Ashdod. A port and industries on these piles of sand? Never! Another guide went through almost the same routine at Arad, describing the proposed development there in the bleak Northern Negev of a major city which would include many industries as well as a center for patients with lung disease. Again, only the politeness due from a guest prevented me from responding with cynical doubt.

But I have visited Ashdod, have walked and driven through its streets, have witnessed its factories and power station and its huge sheltered port. Far from exaggerating, Jerry Avnon had understated what would be done there. By 1974 the city hosted a population of forty thousand, with more than ten thousand children enrolled in its schools. And I have seen Arad, a city designed so that no child need cross a street en route to school, so that no smoke from industry ever blows toward the residential areas. No, I do not doubt. I have seen the impossible happen before in Israel. It will happen again.

In June of 1981 my wife and I were among the ten thousand who, at the Western Wall, heard Elie Wiesel close the Gathering of Holocaust Survivors with these words: "If Auschwitz marked the end of human hope, Jerusalem symbolizes its eternal beginning." This is true for more than Israel, more than Jews. It is true for all humanity.

From this sacred soil came our two most glorious blueprints for human behavior. The prints need no improvement; they are more than enough. From this soil also will yet come a demonstration of how the plans of the Testaments can be implemented. The whole world needs Israel as much as do we Jews.

I will not live to see the Third Testament. But my children's children will. And they will remember that their grandfather said it would be so and did his limited best to help make it so.

14
Faith

A person is more than an aggregate of dates and events. We do not really understand a man or woman just by describing the organizations and causes in which he or she has been engaged. We must inquire also into that individual's ultimate values and ideals. What does he cherish most? How does she view the meaning of her human existence in its cosmic setting? What does she/he consider sacred?

I have quite deliberately deferred to this point any discussion of my spiritual development and where it has brought me. After all, I wasn't born with values or faith. What I believe now is the sum total of all that I have been told or taught, of everything I have experienced and felt from the instant I was conceived into my seventy-eighth year after birth. In a very real sense, then, what I have written so far constitutes the building blocks for my convictions regarding the fundamental meaning of human life.

I commence with the stories of two women whom I tried to help. Everything except their names is true. Jane's voice carried a tone of most desperate urgency. I knew at once this was not a visit that could be deferred a day or even an hour; in twenty minutes I was ringing her doorbell. The maid let me in, ushered me quickly upstairs to her bedroom.

She had already undergone two operations for cancer, was in constant pain, and would reenter the hospital the next day for additional tests to determine the next medical procedure. Her husband was awaiting an available bed for open heart surgery. Small wonder she had wanted me to come over at once. "I remember," she said—her voice punctuated by sobs and moans—"I remember that when my grandmother was dying, she found enormous comfort from her prayerbook, which was never far from her side. I can't pray any more. I can't believe in God if He could torture so mercilessly two people who have always tried to do their best. Why can't I find a faith which will bring me as much confidence and peace as my grandmother's did for her?"

I sat on the couch next to Doris, who was in her thirties, gently holding her hand, listening to her and her father talking tearfully about their wife/mother who had just died. We were planning the funeral service, which was to take place later that day. "What can you say about such a woman?" asked the bereaved husband.

"I can honestly say," I responded, "that she was one of the most beautiful human beings I have ever known. Despite the physical and emotional pain she suffered for years, instead of resenting her lot with bitterness, she could never do enough for others." The daughter roughly yanked her hand away from mine, turned to me almost viciously, and spat out: "Oh yeah—then how come God made her suffer so much?"

Both women were echoing the plaint voiced by Archibald MacLeish's J.B.:

If God is God He is not good,
If God is good He is not God;[1]

At no time does a viable faith become more imperative

than in the face of such tragedy. Never is a rabbi or friend called upon to plumb the depths of conscience and integrity more searchingly. No matter how intellectually satisfying or consistent, a faith that does not respond to the need of the heartbroken and fearful is not worth having.

Traditional theology proposes a panorama of responses:

1. The pain we suffer is punishment for our sins. Thus Job's friends to the most notable of all sufferers. Though he honestly professed his innocence, could not recall any evil he had done to account for such agony, his torment was proof positive that he must have sinned grievously. The divine system of accounting is even more exacting than that of the Internal Revenue Service.

2. God tests us. Even as olives must be squeezed to extract their oil, even as gold is passed through fire to separate pure metal from dross, so God inflicts anguish on us to identify which of us is noble and strong.

3. The inequities so apparent on earth will be corrected in an afterlife. The righteous whom we see suffering will be rewarded there; the wicked who apparently prosper will be punished there. The books will be balanced. In the words of the Mishnah, "This world is but a vestibule for the world to come."

My Aunt Julia, as lonely a spinster as I have ever known, a woman who lived what most people would call a miserable, monotonous life, never complained or feared death. It would not be an exaggeration, as a matter of fact, to say that she was ready to welcome death, convinced, as she was, that God had reserved a seat for her in the next world where she would enjoy eternal bliss at His very side. This was no metaphor for Aunt Julia; she meant and believed it as literal fact. Whatever she had to endure in this life was nothing compared to the joy awaiting her beyond the grave.

4. The relationship between conduct and fate is an impenetrable mystery, beyond the capacity of even the most brilliant human mind to comprehend. We cannot pierce the veil. We must accept the bitterest pain with unquestioning faith. God will not let us down.

Thus far tradition. I cannot accept any of these putative answers. Though it is true that suffering often ennobles character, though I can honestly affirm that almost without exception the finest men and women I have ever known are those who have endured more than their share of misery, I cannot honor or praise a God who resorts to so sadistic a device for the refinement of human character. More than that: if I thought for an instant that God could spare a single child from the agony of Tay-Sachs disease but failed to, if I believed that God could have prevented the Holocaust but, for whatever fiendish or mysterious reasons, chose not to, I would at once renounce the last shred of my religious faith.

How did I come to this conviction?

I have no recollection of theological questions being raised very often in my childhood. I was taught to pray before falling asleep, but no big deal was made of it; that was just the proper way to end the day, much as the proper way to leave a party was to thank my host. God was in a sense taken for granted in our home, assumed to exist without identifying why or how or in what form. Though I could not have known it at the time, in this respect my parents followed the paradigm of Jewish history. In Judaism too, God was assumed, not debated. There is less theological speculation in Jewish thought than in any other religious system I know. Starting with the premise that God exists, the Jew proceeded to cogitate not on what God is

174

like, but on what God expected of him. "What does the Lord require of you? To do justly, to love mercy, to walk humbly with Him." Not to probe into His innermost nature, but *to do*! For us, no endless theorizing as to how many angels could dance on the head of a pin.

I don't recall ever being told as a child that God wanted me to do any particular thing or that He would either punish or reward me. My parents did not use God as a substitute for their own responsibility and effort. As nearly as I can remember, Bible stories were not much of a problem for me, not even those that seemed most improbable or farfetched. Exactly at what age, I don't know, but quite early in life I began to look at these narratives as poetic parables. More important than specific detail as such was the question of what the author of a particular tale was trying to tell or teach.

I was never encouraged to believe that the miracles recorded in the Bible actually took place. I was told, for example, that the parting of the Red Sea (more correctly, the Sea of Reeds) reflected some natural event that our ancestors were unable to understand, hence attributed to God's intervention. Years later an Israeli guide, showing us a very deep *wadi* in the Negev, describing how during the rainy season flash floods frequently rush through these normally dry canyons with such force that many times British troops camping there had been drowned, theorized that it may have been such a *wadi* rather than the sea that Moses and the Israelites crossed in their flight from Egypt. The moment they reached high ground on the other side, an avalanche of water engulfed the Egyptians. My childhood introduction to the Bible made this explanation sound quite plausible. The first time I actually witnessed such a flash-flood, I was even more disposed to accept this interpretation.

The general ambience of my childhood home had

more to do with making me a religious person than any direct indoctrination. Here we come upon what I have long believed is the real etiology of religious faith. If I were asked to define a religious man or woman in psychological rather than theological terms, I would describe a person who trusts the universe. We often fail to realize, however, that for a little child home is the universe. That child's later relationship with God is conditioned on his or her earliest relationship with mother and father. The child reared in a home that can be trusted by loving parents whose discipline is consistent and fair, parents who can forgive without condoning mistakes, who encourage him or her to develop and grow—that child is predisposed to become an adult who trusts the universe, who sees it as a setting compatible with the highest of human aspirations and hopes.

I grew up in such a home. I can remember only one occasion in my entire childhood when either parent lifted a hand against me. I had stolen a few coins from my mother's dresser top, then lied about it when asked. My father used his belt on me. When we joked about it many years later, I could only remotely remember the pain that he still felt.

Aside from that one instance, my parents were loving and fair even when they found it necessary to punish me. I could count on consistent standards by which my conduct would be judged. The *yes* or *no* they voiced on Monday remained *yes* and *no* through the rest of the week. My successes were applauded, my failures criticized without destroying my self-confidence. I was encouraged to grow. Because my home was a trustworthy and congenial place, I came to see the universe as trustworthy and congenial, which means to say I believed and believe in God.

My earliest introduction to religion might have been

less comfortable had I not been so fortunate as never to face in childhood the kind of personal trauma that might have called God into question. My mother died at age eighty, my father at ninety-five. I must have been fourteen or fifteen when my Cleveland grandmother died; my parents—mistakenly, I now think—considered me too young to attend her funeral. The first funeral I ever witnessed was that of my grandfather, who died when I was twenty-one and already engaged in my graduate studies. God did not become an existential problem for me until both my emotional and theological underpinnings had been quite firmly set.

Why did Jane, confronting a possible third cancer operation, find the religious comfort her grandmother had achieved so elusive? More than anything else, I suspect, because she was still operating with pretty much her grandmother's religious concepts and vocabulary. These were good enough for Grandma, no longer adequate for Jane. A major part of my rabbinic concern has been the transposition of eternal religious truths from a key now outmoded and untenable to one more in harmony with today's view of reality. Much of my published writing has been toward that end.

Too many of us exempt religion from the general truth that as our knowledge of reality changes, so our values and behavior must change. We never doubt that in other areas of experience. More than twenty-five years ago, I wrote:

> [People] once believed that by certain kinds of human conduct they could avert the danger of floods. We still believe this today. But where past generations attempted to accomplish this end by performing a variety of rituals and

ceremonies, we do so by conserving forests and building dams. For us to utilize their language and methods would be to prostitute our exalted position in evolution. Yet this is exactly what most of us do in our religious life. Because we have developed a fixation on modes of expression and conceptualization appropriate to earlier and less knowledgeable centuries, we lose sight of the important essence which they expressed in their proper manner and which we must now learn to express in our own way.[2]

The source of such maladjustment is not difficult to discern. Every major religion is premised on the direct, miraculous revelation of truth by God to a favored individual or individuals. Since God Himself was the source, and since God is deemed to be omniscient and perfect, the truth once so revealed is considered to be changeless.

But is this in very fact the way our religious systems originated? Would it not be more accurate to say that they were first conceived on earth, then reached for heaven? Human beings lived on this planet a long time before religion came into existence. They observed (a) the various forms of life around them; (b) the orderly, mostly predictable procedures of nature; (c) their relationships with other persons; and (d) their own inner feelings and fears, frustrations and hopes. Out of all this in the long course of time, men and women arrived at certain convictions and values. To be sure, they then invariably attributed the resultant truths to divine revelation. But the fact is that millennia of human experience came first.

Perhaps two simple diagrams can elucidate the difference. The older, still more common view can be represented thus:

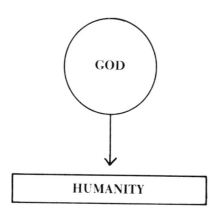

Here is the newer, I think more realistic understanding of the process:

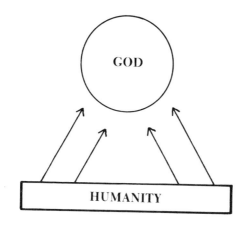

Just as there are these two approaches to the origins of religion, so are there two basic ways of formulating our faith. The first is carefully to catalogue our most fundamental human needs, then to project tenets of faith that meet these needs. The second adds a most important ingredient. Commencing also with our existential needs, it gives equal consideration to the nature of reality, insofar as we are capable of knowing and understanding reality. To be acceptable, then, as a postulate of faith, a given belief must not only satisfy our most imperative needs *but also square with the real world.*

An example: It would certainly fulfill a most urgent need for me to believe that, if I have faith in God and pray regularly and act ethically and observe a regimen of traditional Jewish ritual, my family and I will be spared all major illness. But I can accept that only by closing my eyes to fact. I do in truth have faith in God. I do pray regularly and act ethically and practice Jewish ritual as we Reform Jews understand it. So did my first wife. None of this, however, prevented her suffering recurrent major illness— first emotional, then physical too—over a period of more than two decades, culminating in nearly six years of debilitating hospitalization before she finally died. For me to accept Aunt Julia's kind of faith, the kind that seeks only to satisfy my crying need, without regard to its consonance with reality and fact, would be absurd.

I sat one day with a young physician who had been indicted for alleged Medicare fraud. At least in the sanctity of my study, he did not deny his guilt. Both he and his wife were in tears as he protested, "Why doesn't God help me? Why have I come to religious services all these years and tried to be a good Jew if God won't help me when I need Him?"

It would have been altogether reasonable for this man

to expect that his faith in God might impel him to act honestly in the first place. Even that such faith would now give him strength to endure what he must and to improve his behavior in the future. Such expectations square with reality. To conceive God, however, as a Cosmic Lone Ranger, who can gallop in on command to save us from the consequences of our own mistakes—this, at its best, is childish illusion.

In one sense I am a pragmatist, in another sense not. I am convinced that in order to be valid, a system of religious belief must perform certain definite functions. These are to explain the universe, give meaning to our individual and collective lives, help us survive the inevitable bumps and blows all of us must expect to suffer, and motivate us to higher levels of ethical action. I am not a pragmatist, however, to the extent of agreeing that any faith that serves these functions thereby qualifies automatically as true. It must also sit well with the facts of existence.

What I have been struggling to say, though the precise words have yet to be used, is that faith must be consistent with fact, religion with science. This is not so new or revolutionary a thought as it may at first seem to be. Our ancestors' faith was consistent with their "science," which means to say, what they believed was consistent with the facts of reality as they perceived them. Throughout the long course of religious development, changes in knowledge inevitably led to changes in belief and practice.

You can illustrate this as easily as I. Once it was accepted that a variety of gods controlled nature and human destiny. As we learned more about the pervasive unity inhering within reality, all but the most primitive of religions moved toward faith in one God. Once religious men and women were convinced that the only way to reverse the annual threat of the sun's disappearing as winter's days grew shorter and shorter was to light huge fires, to dance around them while chanting magic incantations. As we learned more about nature's autonomous patterns, the fires of December, transmuted into the lights of Chanukah and Christmas, were given historical and/or theological meanings. Faith in one God rather than many, the idea that days would grow longer even without our magical supplications—these adaptations to newer insights and knowledge were no less radical and disturbing when originally proposed than some of my new religious interpretations today.

Early one beautiful morning, we stood together in a circle on a luxuriant lawn. Attending a national conference at a rural camp, we had gathered before breakfast to greet the new day with prayer. The setting was indescribably magnificent. Only a dullard or dolt would fail to feel God's presence. Then my young colleague who was conducting the service spoiled it all. Directing us to a page in the prayerbook more expressive of the fifteenth century than the twentieth, he said, "Let's read these words aloud. Even if you don't believe them, read them!"

There's the crux of the matter. When we read or recite words we don't really believe—however fervently—we make a mockery of what should be precious.

By its very nature, faith will always go beyond fact. But it must commence with fact, be consistent with fact. I believe many things I cannot possibly know. I cannot believe anything that I am sure is impossible or absurd. Albert Einstein saw his work as "reaching to the rim of the sun, unravelling some of God's tightly held secrets, bringing them down to earth and setting them gently down before the peoples of the earth." This is as fine a way as I know of expressing what should be the relationship between science and religion.

For me, there has never been a conflict between the two. Indeed, I have often been more inspired by the writings of perceptive scientists than by those of the most eminent theologians. Forgive me for saying that I sometimes find more relevant religious conviction and insight in the words of Julian Huxley and Edmund Sinnott than in those of Paul Tillich or Franz Rosenzweig. The theologians who have influenced me most are men like Mordecai Kaplan and Milton Steinberg, who never ask me to be a spiritual schizophrenic, to divorce what I believe from what I know.

When Temple Israel of Boston was planning its new synagogue building in the early 1970s, I was eager to include a symbolic expression of the integral relationship between religion and science. To that end, I spent a great deal of time with our architects and artists. I remembered that in Israel's Ben Shemen Youth Village, the Holy Ark is flanked by two of Albert Einstein's early scientific instruments, which he personally bequeathed to the villagers. The man who designed our Ark doors included on them a combination of sharp, angular lines representing science and of soft, curving surfaces expressing the warmth and emotion of faith. Each needs the other for completion. In similar manner, Louise Nevelson's monumental exterior sculpture near the building's main entrance depicts in her inimitable style the indispensability of science for religion and of religion for science.

In a sense, this entire chapter is preface. It prepares us to inquire now into the specifics of my faith, how they may have changed through the years, how they function in my life. And how they may be helpful in yours.

15

God

It would be ideal if I could now retrace in my personal religious development the steps taken by humanity at large in its slow, stumbling progress toward more refined religious ideas and values. To start with a clean slate, inscribe on it successive intellectual and emotional impressions, finally to add them all up, arriving at my current convictions and conclusions. Ideal, but impossible. Long before I was able to observe my universe in any but the most superficial sense, my parents had begun to convey to me, even if only indirectly, the distilled essence of what Jewish tradition had concluded as refracted through themselves. It is no longer possible for me neatly to separate what I was told from what I observed for myself. The best I can hope to do now is to examine what I believe in the light of what we know, to discern whether or not the two are compatible.

First, a word of warning. A friend who teaches Jewish thought has accused me of granting higher priority to science than to Jewish religious tradition. Instead of utilizing science to judge the validity of Judaism, he proposes, I ought to use Judaism by which to test science. Is it true that my way of thinking bestows higher priority on fact than on faith? I say *no*. By way of analogy, I have suggested to my friend, let us assume that I wish to make the finest, tastiest chicken soup I can. Toward that end, at a certain stage in the process I use a strainer to eliminate vegetable and bones, thus creating a purer broth.

Have I assigned highest priority to the strainer? Not really. My most important purpose remains the cooking of a delicious soup. The strainer is used as an instrument toward attaining that goal. So it is, I firmly believe, with science and religion. Science is the strainer. Religion remains my highest, topmost priority.

With this in mind, where do I begin? Perhaps the best starting point is the single most important sentence in all of Judaism, a declaration frequently referred to as its watchword. I mean, of course, the *Shema*: "Hear, O Israel, the Eternal is our God, the Eternal alone!" We Jews recite or sing this affirmation so often—at every public service of worship, as conclusion for our private prayers, wherever possible as our final avowal before death—that we are apt to concentrate less on meaning than on rote. So let us take a fresh look.

What does it mean to affirm the unity and uniqueness of God? Does it not imply a unity and uniqueness to all His works? In order for God truly to be one, the universe must be one; each of us within himself or herself must be one; all of us together must be one; we and the universe must be one. Like an identifiable motif, woven through every part of a multi-colored design, holding the whole thing together, there must be a unifying theme binding together every seemingly disparate part of the cosmos, including ourselves.

And this is precisely, exquisitely what science teaches today! What our ancestors could only have suspected through some uncanny kind of intuition, we now know as confirmed fact. Thus the universe is indeed one. The very same chemical elements that constitute my body have been identified as components of all physical entities to the outermost reaches of space. The periodic table, which reflects the relationship of these elements to each other here on earth, is valid for the entire universe. The rotation of invisible particles within the table on which I type follows the very patterns and proportions of the planets, moving about their respective suns. Indeed, our universe is one!

We ourselves are both product and part of this unity. We are not detached observers. As we study the stars, in a sense we are studying ourselves. We are made of the same stuff, governed by the same laws, products of the same plan. We are nature grown conscious of itself. In a way far more precise than the most ecstatic of mystics could have guessed, the planets and clouds and trees are my brothers.

This means that the potentiality of everything we have become or may yet be was present at the inception of the universe. The possibilty—perhaps inevitability—of the organic was present in the inorganic, of the conscious in the unconscious, of the moral in the amoral, of the spiritual in the crudely physical. This is as true in the larger sense as it is true that the potentiality of the flower inheres in its seed, that the nature of the sea can be surmised by studying a single drop.

Show a scientist two drops of water; he will immediately identify which came from the ocean, which from a lake. Give him an apple, a peach, and a pear; he will know at once precisely the kind of tree from which each was picked. This is so because the part must be consistent with its whole. Each automatically and ineluctably reveals the essence of the other.

Let me try to say the same thing differently. *Appleness* must exist in the very nature of a tree that produces apples. Salinity must characterize an ocean whose drops consist of salt water. A great Jewish thinker named Bachya said it many centuries ago: "Study man, and when we arrive at an understanding of him, much of the mystery of the universe will be clear to us." So, in order to learn more about overall existence, let us study ourselves. We are to the cosmos as the apple is to the tree, as the drop is to the sea.

That we are physical organisms, akin to and emergent from other physical organisms that preceded us on this planet, is by now common knowledge. But, unlike our biological predecessors, we are also spiritual beings. I define spiritual as the opposite of physical—the intangible, impalpable, trans-physical part of us. Our brains are physical; our minds—our philosophies, ideas, thoughts—are spiritual. Our glands and their secretions are physical; our emotions and aspirations, our conscience and yearning for beauty, these are spiritual. True, we cannot conceive of mind without brain, of emotion without glands. But they are not identical. The physical produces the spiritual; the spiritual emerges from the physical.

I define soul as our superiority over other forms of earthly life: the capacity to create and appreciate truth, beauty, and moral goodness. And I am convinced that this, no less than our hands or brains, evolved from our primeval beginnings, was a potentiality of the universe at its inception.

Time now to extrapolate from us to the universe. Remember: The purpose of studying ourselves was to learn more about our cosmic setting. If a propensity for truth, beauty, and moral goodness exists in us, something like it must have pre-existed us. The spiritual raw materials for the human enterprise, no less than its physical elements, had to be traits of the universe before the first of our species could appear.

An oxygen-breathing creature could not have developed in a universe devoid of oxygen. The eye could not have evolved in a universe lacking light waves, nor the ear in an environment without sound waves. We are reflections of, reactions to the nature of that which produced us, which means that an animal with a soul could not have emerged unless there were spiritual as well as physical reality inherent in our universe.

The innate spiritual essence of the cosmos is what I call God. God is the Seed of the universe. God is the Dynamic, the Potential, the Thrust of the universe. God is the Soul of the universe, a magnification to infinity of what we call soul in ourselves.

As shocking as this may seem to some of my readers, it need not be so. It does not represent a total, absolute break with the past. If we thoughtfully reconsider what our ancestors were trying to teach, rephrase their truths in a vocabulary consistent with our own time, then extend their understandings in accordance with our greater insight and knowledge, we shall find more consistency and continuity than we may at first suspect. It would come out something like this:

1. This universe, far from being a colossal accident or series of coincidents, reflects pervasive order, purpose, plan.

2. Our human lives are an integral part of this plan.

3. Far from being completed, this cosmic plan is still in ferment, still thrusting toward the future.

4. Up to the human level—as mentioned in an earlier chapter—God was Himself in total charge of the entire process. He was, so to speak, the Energizer within evolution. The life forms through which Divine Energy flowed were unconscious instruments in a process of which they knew nothing. My cat or dog is just as essential a step in the process as I am, but is entirely oblivious to all of it.

5. As human beings, we are agents, not instruments; aware, not unconscious. We can promote the process . . . or

retard it . . . or even demolish and foreclose it. We are God's partners in the implementation of His plan. He has yielded a share of His responsibility to us. He needs us almost as much as we need Him.

6. As we thus strive to cooperate with God, He remains a very vital part of the process, both "out there" and here within ourselves. He is not the Retired Architect of the Universe. He is the Spiritual Component in cosmic reality, endorsing and reinforcing our best efforts. He is not like a strong wind, blowing the inert log inevitably toward a predetermined destination; rather like an incalculable Source of Energy, which will help us if we are aware of it and know how to cooperate with it.

William P. Montague came as close as anyone to expressing the essential verities of religious truth, flowing from the past, through the present, toward the future:

> Religion is not merely a belief in an ultimate reality or in an ultimate ideal. . . . Religion is a momentous possibility, the possibility namely that what is highest in spirit is also deepest in nature—that there is something at the heart of nature, something akin to us, a conserver and increaser of values . . . that the things that matter most are not at the mercy of the things that matter least.

Is there inherent purpose to our human lives? The existentialist says *no*; we ourselves must supply the purpose; objectively, it doesn't exist. I say *yes*; there is intrinsic purpose in the process of life itself. When we are exposed to suffering, this may be the most crucial question of all. For the person who perceives a purpose being served by pain can endure a much higher degree of agony than one who suffers in a void. I made passing reference to this in an earlier chapter. If I know that the aches following upon surgery serve the purpose of prolonging my life—or better yet, of providing a kidney to save the life of one I love—the level of my tolerance for pain will be ever so much higher than if I have just carelessly slipped on ice and broken my hip.

A comparison of World War II veterans with those who fought in Vietnam can be very instructive in this respect. Studies have clearly established that the latter group experienced a much greater degree of criminality, of mental illness, of drug abuse than the former. For me, there is no mystery in this. Surely the horrors endured by both groups were comparable. We who fought in World War II, however, had little reason to doubt that an abiding purpose was being served. The preservation of freedom, the sacredness of human life, the survival of the Jewish people—all these were at stake. Many of those who warred in Vietnam, on the other hand—perhaps most of them—saw themselves as helpless pawns in a maelstrom without meaning or aim.

As a Marine Corps chaplain, I officiated at what may have been the first or perhaps even the only marriage ceremony uniting two Jewish Marines. Less than a year later, I had to inform the bride that her husband had been killed in combat. Her response read in part as follows: "My only thought and prayer now is that Marty's death was not in vain. He held his ideals very high and was willing to die for them; should they ever be destroyed, I would lose all faith and trust in humanity." The only kind of suffering that even the strongest are unable to survive is that which serves no purpose.

What, then, is the pervasive purpose of the human enterprise? To assist God in the further advancement of life through evolution. The most significant progress from now on will be spiritual more than physical. This is precisely the area in which we human beings can contribute most. Because we are equipped to contribute most, we also of necessity suffer most. The same delicate, sensitive nervous structure that enables us to compose symphonies, to paint portraits, to experience love, also exposes us to more deeply excruciating dimensions of pain. These pains are the price we must pay for being God's partners in pushing the course of evolution still higher. We could avoid them only by settling for the status of senseless robots or dull clods.

I have no choice whether to suffer. I do have other choices, chiefly how to interpret and endure my suffering. Each time that I opt for truth instead of falsehood, for beauty rather than ugliness, for righteousness in place of evil, I have given perspective to my pain by saying *yes* to life and to God.

16
Today

Anyone who believes in God as a Divine Daddy, as one who can, if He wishes, respond favorably to every human petition, has no problem with prayer. Can a naturalistic religionist, who eschews miracles, who does not believe that God will or can suspend the laws of nature in response to human wishes, can such a person pray? The easiest existential answer is: yes. I know so because I am such an individual and I pray at least once every day. Why? What does prayer mean to me? What do I expect to achieve through prayer? To answer all these questions, let me enunciate my understanding of prayer in a series of statements, each really saying pretty much the same as the others but in slightly different form:

—Prayer is the reinforcement of my relationship with the Soul of the universe, thus to realize a greater measure of my spiritual potential.

—Prayer is a reminder of who I am, of what I can become, of how I fit into the universal scheme of things.

—Prayer is an inventory of the spiritual resources that nature has invested in me and of how I can exploit them to their fullest.

—Prayer is any intellectual, emotional, or aesthetic experience that seeks or strengthens my spiritual relationship with the universe.

The purpose of prayer is not to change God or His cosmos; it is rather to change me. The function of prayer is to facilitate my adjustment to reality, not to cajole reality into matching my desires or needs. God is present whether I pray or not. God performs His necessary work in sustaining and conserving the universe whether I pray or not. My words of prayer can in no way alter God or change His posture; they can alter only me.

Because this is not yet by any means the common perception of prayer, I have through the years created my own supplementary worship services for use by the two congregations I have served. My effort was always directed toward combining the traditional with the new. As I approached each Hebrew passage in the liturgy, I asked these questions: (a) What were our ancestors really attempting to say here? (b) Of the truths they thus proclaimed, which are still valid for us? (c) How can we say the same thing, using a lexicon more congenial to our time and need?

So here are my current views: on God, on religion and science, on prayer. Here they are, much as I expressed them a quarter-century ago in *Man's Best Hope*. Have they changed during the intervening years? To some extent, yes, but less than I might have expected. I reread *Man's Best Hope* in preparation for the writing of the last chapter and this one. Let me confess—whatever immodesty is thus disclosed—that I am pleased with it. On page after page, I found myself nodding in vigorous assent, saying: "Yes, that's exactly what I meant; I would still express it in much the same way." In a mood of silly self-approval, I remarked to my wife: "You know, if someone else had written this paragraph, I would probably be quoting it." Yet there have been changes, even if more in emphasis than substance.

I was a rationalist then; I remain essentially a rationalist now. I was a religious naturalist then; I am scarcely less so now. My faith was grounded in scientific fact then; it still is. But I have learned that reason and science—however imperative they both are—cannot in and of themselves suffice.

I possessed considerable theoretical knowledge when first formulating my adult theological perspectives. I hadn't yet suffered enough, however, to know that in moments of most acute pain the heart cries out for a God greater than the mind may ever be able to comprehend. I still cannot believe in a God whom science and reason show to be impossible or absurd. If I have changed, it's in sometimes needing and accepting a God whom neither science nor reason may ever be able to touch. More than in earlier years, I see now in religion a larger place for emotion, for intuition, perhaps even for a minor measure of mysticism.

Yet, as I have already confessed, mysticism as the major ingredient of religion frightens me. If the cold, sharp blade of reason, unsheathed by emotion and feeling, can give us Nietzsche or even Hitler, naked mysticism produces Jim Jones and the Moonies. A young colleague of mine—bright, compassionate, sensitive—is much more a mystic than I. He has described to me how, when once in imminent danger of death, he momentarily felt as if he were floating above the scene of accident, observing himself without fear. At the very moment of terrifying peril, he felt the most profound sense of peacefulness he had ever known. If I did not love and respect him so much, I might be inclined to suspect his sanity. In the past I most probably would have yielded to cynicism despite my affection and respect.

Today the thought flashes through my mind: Perhaps he has experienced something that has eluded me. Perhaps extrasensory perception and similar manifestations of mysticism are on the growing edge of evolutionary development, pointing the way toward the next stage in life's irresistible thrust upward. There was a time in the process of evolution when only a few fish—for what reason no one of us knows—had begun to develop the swim bladders that later became lungs, the strong, underbelly fins that were destined to be limbs. They pointed toward the future, toward the possibility of life on dry land. Perhaps my young friend now points toward a future that I can visualize little more than fish could anticipate my writing this book. The very fact that I can now say *perhaps* marks a significant, even if subtle change in my theology.

Yet I must return to my discomfort with mysticism. It pains me—at times unbearably—to witness the extent to which intellect and mind are condemned today in some religious circles. Unadulterated mysticism is nearly always a rejection of intellect and mind. I think I understand why this contamination of rational thought has occurred. The stresses and strains of life, on both personal and societal levels, are sometimes more than even the strongest of us can handle. We yearn for a daddy, human or divine, who will answer all our questions, resolve all our doubts, assuage all our hurts. Hence the cults. Hence the resurgence of evangelical Christianity and chassidic Judaism. Hence—to me most discouraging and disappointing of all—the repudiation of mind even by some Jews who no longer expect their children to read or study, who overemphasize the importance of feeling at the expense of knowing, who bastardize Judaism as they compete with the cults for easy, salvational answers.

I am of two minds. On the one hand, I cannot any longer be so smug as to reject mysticism totally. On the other, I consider my capacity for thought to be one of God's greatest gifts. Not to use it to its utmost would be an inexcusable waste of a most precious natural resource.

196

There have been other changes in my theology also. I see more room and need now than I once did for prayer as an expression of our most desperately urgent anguish. As with Job. As with the Psalmist. We know that one of psychotherapy's most valuable tools is the creation of an atmosphere in which a troubled individual can—without fear of criticism or guilt—express whatever hurts him or her most. Free ventilation itself can be a large part of the cure. There are times when our hearts are so heavy that they require more than even the most sympathetic of human responses. At such times we must cry out to the universe, to God. I did so in my Iwo foxhole. Not that I expected God to intervene by diverting the course of a bullet or shell headed my way. But the pressure of fear mounting in my heart and gut had to be released.

I voiced such prayer also while my father was slowly dying, when my first wife was in human terms already dead even though her heart was still beating, and for my dearest friend who was senile in a nursing home for several years before his death. In no case did I beg God to suspend His own laws of nature. I asked that if it could happen within these laws, the patient be cured; that if not, he or she remain comfortable, that final release come as speedily as possible. And I asked in my prayers whether there was anything that either the doctors or I could do that we had forgotten.

My prayers saved neither my father, Jack Rudin, nor Ruth. But they gave me needed comfort by reminding me that my loved ones and I are equal participants in God's plan, that a Healing Power works in their bodies and minds as well as in mine—a Power that always "tries" though it cannot always succeed. And that the same Comforting and Strengthening Power can help me confront my apprehensions of both present and future.

Another way in which my approach to prayer has changed: I can now confess, as I could not have done earlier in life, that despite my rejection of older, outmoded frames of reference, despite my newer, more sophisticated ways of thinking, I often pray *as if* God were a listening Person. There is at best—let me say it once and for all—there is an inevitable, ineradicable gap between head and heart.

I don't think I ever acknowledged this even to myself until it blurted itself out as I was writing this paragraph. I have always been allergic to anthropomorphic expressions about God. As an educator, I have insisted that God not be called Father, that children not be encouraged or even allowed to conceive God as a human being. While that still is my ultimate perspective, I realize now that with little children the battle is lost before it is even begun; it fails to account for the fact that up to a certain age we all anthropomorphize everything. Four-year-olds talk to a door, a table, a chair—all as if they were persons. Is it reasonable to forbid them from talking to God as if He too were a person?

What moved me most to yield on this point was a letter from a close friend who happened to be a psychoanalyst. He described how his mother tried to avoid giving her children an anthropomorphic image of God. She told them, pointing upward, that God is everywhere and that He can see everything we do. My friend remembered that as a child he identified God with a revolving chimney atop a building across from their Viennese apartment. It was near heaven, where his mother had pointed, and, "looking" in all directions, it would "see" everything. I'm afraid it's inevitable: children will conceive God in human terms no matter what we do; our aim must be to move them away from such notions as soon as they are ready to be so moved.

I recall the time that a little seven-year-old girl asked: "Rabbi, how can we tell when God is near us?" "Betty dear," I said, "have you ever seen a flower so beautiful that you couldn't take your eyes off it?" No, Betty could not remember ever seeing a flower that beautiful. My first effort having failed, I tried again: "Have you ever seen autumn trees dressed in so many gorgeous colors that you had to catch your breath when you saw them?" This time I was more successful. Betty did indeed remember such trees, and proceeded to tell me with great excitement how she went walking with her daddy and the trees were so beautiful she was sorry when night came and she could no longer see them.

I explained: "Betty, you knew God was near you then, because God made the trees so beautiful, and God made you feel happy when you saw them." In like manner, I tried to help Betty understand that when she does something good, God is in the warm feeling she enjoys inside herself. And when she does something wrong, God is in her uncomfortable feeling. I did not try to tell her what God is like. I do not know that myself; how could I tell her? What I do know as an adult is that for me God is the Source of and the Urge toward the good, the beautiful and the true. So I tried to identify Him with whatever of the good, the beautiful, and the true Betty could understand. I did not attempt to make God seem concrete, rather to identify Him with aspects of life that bridge the concrete and abstract, which could seem real even to a little child. Betty, I hope, will not confuse God with a chimney.

Will my modern theology meet the needs of every religious individual in this twentieth century? Of course not. An extremely intelligent woman who has heard me expostulate on God many times responds: "I understand

199

your thinking and admire it. But I must be honest in telling you that I seek a different kind of God, a personal God who is close to me, as my parents were when I was a child." I would not argue with this woman even if she were not my wife. Her religious needs differ from mine; her solutions must therefore also diverge from mine.

I have already suggested that the proper functions of religion are to explain existence, to infuse meaning into our lives, to help us negotiate the rough spots that can otherwise destroy us, to move us toward a higher level of ethical action. Any faith that serves these functions in an individual's life, which he or she does not try to force upon others and which hurts no one, is, so far as I am concerned, a legitimate faith for that person.

Were my ideas helpful to Jane and Doris, whose pathos was described earlier? I can only hope so, I do not know. For one thing, unless pressed beyond resistance, I never discuss theology under the immediate impact of pain or grief. I said earlier that the time to prepare for tragedy is before it appears. The way to deal with a fatal disease caused by vitamin deficiency is to provide the necessary vitamins in advance, not frantically to swallow huge quantities of pills after the disease has struck. I believe in preventive theology as well as preventive medicine. This is why I always included extensive discussions on tragedy and suffering in my high-school confirmation classes.

What theological preparation would I want for Jane and Doris? First, the idea that even God's power is limited. Indeed, this is precisely what I suggested to Doris. "God didn't *make* Mother suffer," I said. "He was unable to prevent it. There are some things that even God cannot do."

I thought at that moment—though I refrained from mentioning it—of Frances Gunther's wonderful remark after her brilliant fifteen-year-old son had died of brain cancer: "I did not . . . feel that God had personally singled out either him or us for any special act either of animosity or generosity. . . . " Speaking of the doctors, she said: "They were helpless, and we were helpless, and in His way, God, standing by us in our hour of need . . . was helpless to."[1]

God possesses all the power there is, more power than everyone and everything else combined. But there are limits even to His vast power. There are hopes that even He cannot fulfill.

"It would be wonderful," I continued in my effort to console Doris, "if good people were always rewarded for their admirable behavior. But life just doesn't work that way. Often it seems unfair, but it's true: sometimes the finest men and women we know are the ones who suffer most."

Had this young woman ever been in one of my classes she might have remembered at that point my comments about two kinds of Natural Law, physical and spiritual. She could have recalled my conclusion that physical Natural Law operates without regard for a person's righteousness or its opposite. If two individuals, the most righteous and the most wicked in the world, simultaneously fell from a skyscraper roof, the law of gravity would play upon both of them exactly the same. The spiritual Natural Law, operating through their consciences, would make distinctions; the physical Law would not.

We do not know the cause of cancer, the culprit afflicting both of the women I described. God gave us enough intelligence to discover both cause and cure, but we have squandered it in a morbid, obscene quest for better ways to kill more people in less time. That isn't God's fault, it's ours.

Where, then, is God? If He cannot always save or spare

us, what good is He? God is the Strength that enables us to survive catastrophe. God is the Love that helps us transpose our own pain into blessing for others. God is the Healing tht makes it possible to surmount our most devastating losses and eventually even to smile again.

Could such thoughts—if they had become absorbed and digested at an earlier moment—have helped Doris and Jane? I *hope* so. I *know* they have helped others. A woman whom I had never met stopped to introduce herself at a wedding reception. "I was in the audience five months ago," she said, "when you lectured on your kind of religious faith. You had no way of knowing that I was about to undergo surgery, the prospect of which almost immobilized me with fright. You helped me put the pieces together that night. Your words entered the hospital with me, were as effective as any medicine prescribed by my doctors. You helped me understand that I am part of something much bigger and more important than myself; that there is a Healing Power working within me; that I must do my share, meet my responsibilities, for that Power to succeed. I couldn't leave here tonight without thanking you."

My modern, naturalistic theology worked for her. It has certainly worked for me. It helped when I had to make the choice between pacifism and the chaplaincy. It helped on Iwo in conquering my faintness at the sight of blood. It helped many times when the American Legion and the press and some of my own congregants resented my stand on controversial moral issues. It helped me meet my responsibilities to Ruth as well as myself during her long, agonizing illness. It helped me reconstruct my life after her death, accept and enjoy a new, guiltless happiness with the wife who now blesses each minute of every day. In all these monumental crises, my new kind of faith opened for me a vista of the higher purpose I was meant to serve, of the inner resources that reflect the Great Cosmic Resource called God.

Notes

1. John Gunther, *Death Be Not Proud* (Harper & Row, 1949), p. 252. Copyright 1949 by John Gunther. Used by permission of Harper & Row, Publishers, Inc.

17

Hope

So . . . *here am I!*

Where? In the evening of my career as rabbi, writer, lecturer. Though technically retired from congregational pulpit duties, I still officiate on occasion for weddings, funerals, Bar and Bat Mitzvah ceremonies when requested to do so by congregants who have remained close to me. I still counsel the troubled, though nowhere near as extensively as I once did. My participation in national and worldwide Zionist leadership brings me to Israel frequently. Invitations to lecture and to serve as scholar-in-residence for various congregations cover an arc spanning California and Jerusalem via Florida and South Africa. It gives me much pleasure to joke that most men retire to get *off* the road. For years I have said, only half facetiously, "I want to die the day before I awaken in the morning to wonder: 'What on God's earth will I do today?'"

I never yield to sleep at night without thanking God for blessings beyond counting: for genetic stamina and good health; for parents who, far from coddling or stifling me, taught me to stand on my own feet physically, spiritually, and emotionally; for a sister who loves me dearly despite her knowledge of my faults; for wonderful friends to sustain me in my moments of despair; for children and grandchildren who love me for my virtues and tease me about my deficiencies; for two congregations that have aggravated me enough to keep me from becoming stodgy, while respecting me and following my leadership enough to stimulate my creativity.

And most of all, for Ruth and Hulda. Ruth, without whose help I could never have built three-score families into a congregation of more than nine hundred. Ruth, whose warmth made friends of men and women who might otherwise have resented me for the standards I stubbornly imposed upon them. Ruth, who in love bore the son and daughter whom I treasure more each day. If, in the end, she failed, it was not for lack of trying, nor because there was evil in her. Only because she had never been given a decent chance to grow beyond emotional childhood. The most compassionate love and support I was capable of giving her, even when coupled with the skills of her several psychiatrists, were not enough to divert her from the womb to which she was determined to return. Tragically, from this womb, unlike the first in which she had been conceived, there was no opening into birth.

And for Hulda, without whom it would make no difference to me whether I lived or died. For Hulda, who tenderly picked up the broken shards and fashioned them into another life for me. For Hulda, who suffered as much pain in her way as I did in mine: losing mother, father, first husband and both brothers to cruelest death; yet recovering from her own despair to bestow the most generous and nourishing kind of love I have ever witnessed on all who come close to her. Especially on me.

What brought me here? A career of ample fulfillment. I remember, during my final year at the Hebrew Union College, responding to the challenge of my favorite uncle, who found it difficult to understand my choice of profession. I had worked in his retail store one summer and had apparently impressed him with my business ability. "Roland," he said, "you would be good in any business; why in the world would you want to follow a line of work which will bring you so many kinds of trouble without giving you anywhere near the income you could otherwise make?" My answer—quaint and naive as it sounds now—was utterly honest: "Uncle Lew, all I want in life is to do work which I find both interesting and useful, and eventually to earn five thousand dollars a year." It goes without saying that in 1936 the sum I mentioned would have provided much more than it would now.

Has the first part of my expectation, the quality of work I sought, been realized? More than I would then have dared expect! I look upon myself as a general practioner in the rabbinate. Every phase of my professional activity appeals to me: study, reading, preaching, writing, teaching, communal leadership, counseling—all without exception. My principal complaint has been that there aren't enough hours in the day or days in a week to do as much of each as I might have wanted.

My summers have been spent for the most part in writing. The dozen published books bearing my name—all but one written on the porch of the lakeside New Hampshire cottage where this is being typed—have given me welcome relief from the pressure-cooker that might otherwise have consumed me. I think, incidentally, that holding the first copy of his own published book is the closest a man can come to his wife's experience of coddling her newborn child.

Nothing has pleased me more than working with my rabbinical colleagues, with the lay-leaders of American Reform Judaism, and on the bridge binding them together. Titles and honors have never meant much to me; an assortment of testimonial plaques gathers dust on one shelf of my study closet. The one position I unabashedly wanted from the day of my ordination was the Presidency of the

Central Conference of American Rabbis. Another, which I least expected, was to serve as a Vice-Chairman of the Board in the Union of American Hebrew Congregations. More gratifying even than these—as I look back on more than half a century—is the confidence many of my colleagues evidenced in coming to me for professional counseling and in accepting me on numerous occasions to arbitrate conflict between their congregations and themselves.

And my congregants? I have infuriated and threatened some, encouraged and inspired others by my pronounced stand on issues of public morality. My guess is that very few members of my congregation have felt neutral toward me; my kind of personality engenders vigorous support or bitter opposition, seldom mild indifference. In the nineteenth century, Rabbi Israel Salanter said: "A rabbi whose community does not disagree with him is no rabbi; a rabbi who fears his community is no man."

The pressures and problems of a rabbinical career proved to be far heavier than I could possibly have anticipated. But so have the satisfactions and fulfillments greatly exceeded my expectations. I claim no sympathy. I would make the same professional choice again.

Which were my most serious mistakes? If I had my life to live over, would I do better?

Mistakes there were, of course. Especially in my younger professional years, I could have been less stubborn, more tolerant of alternatives, quicker to accept compromise. I should have evaded the delusion that my presence was essential at every public function, in favor of spending more time with my family. While I think I did reasonably well in my treatment of individuals face-to-face, often in speaking out on public issues I was less sensitive than I might have been to the problems and needs of my congregants. Many of the individual business people in the

207

congregation, for example, were not guilty of the immoralities and malfeasances I frequently condemned. They faced worries and anxieties, moreover, of which I was often unaware.

I have little difficulty identifying what I believe to be my most serious rabbinic deficiency. Notwithstanding the excessively flattering introductions inflicted on me as a speaker, I know that I am not a scholar. A perpetual student, I hope; clearly not a scholar. At best my graduate studies could provide me with no more than a foundation for scholarship. Because of my deep interest in every practical aspect of the rabbinate, I never built adequately on that foundation. Too much of my subsequent research, therefore, was done through secondary sources and translations rather than originals.

On ethical matters, I'm satisfied that performance has at least come close to matching intention. Yet there have been lapses, some reaching back many years, which continue to bother me. They always involved gnawing conflicts of values. Did I resolve them properly or just conveniently? A high official of my congregation was indicted on a criminal charge. Because I was beholden to him personally as a close friend, I agreed to testify on his behalf, without really knowing enough about the case to be sure.

A merchant-congregant from whom I was making a substantial purchase offered a professional discount but asked to be paid in cash. Could there have been any reason for such a request other than tax evasion? Yet I complied without asking questions.

Would I do better if given another chance? I doubt it. Yes, I would probably avoid or correct some of my acknowledged mistakes. But then being human—therefore fallible—I would make others.

Could I have come any other way? Is my feeling of freedom only a cruel but comfortable illusion? Yes, I could have come other ways. No, the freedom I prize is not an illusion. I cannot prove this, yet I firmly believe it with every fibre of my being. I cannot prove that my wife is more sensitive to my needs and more supportive in meeting them than any other person on earth. I cannot prove God. Yet these are firm foundations on which my entire existence is built. So is the conviction that I am free.

Not entirely free, of course not. Unaided by any mechanical contraption, I can neither breathe under water nor fly through the air. I am bound by the laws of nature. When playing gin-rummy, I am limited by the hand I hold. When flying a kite, I must reckon with the direction and intensity of the wind. But I can play my hand poorly or well, fly my kite to take advantage of the wind or to let it thwart me. So, in the adventure of life—restricted, admittedly, by nature's rules—I can choose between right and left, between up and down, between good and evil.

Many are the shackles by which I am allegedly enslaved: genes, instincts, my unconscious; environment, economics, my fate. How foolish to deny that all of them—except perhaps the last, in which I do not believe—in some ways limit my freedom. But how short-sighted and narrow to conclude that they have stripped me of all freedom.

I have seen too many men and women rise magnificently above all these oppressive forces that were supposed to keep them down ever to believe for an instant that human freedom is illusory. One Helen Keller, one Albert Schweitzer, one Leo Baeck is all the argument I need to reject an easy surrender to fate.

When the Hebrew Union College–Jewish Institute of Religion first opened its Jerusalem school, the cantor who officiated at religious services was a German refugee. He

209

and his family were on board a freight train carrying its terrified human cargo toward an extermination oven. It happened to have been in late December. At one stop several SS officers opened the door to inquire whether any of the passengers could sing. Others pointed to the cantor. His wife and children remained on the train, continuing their fateful journey to the crematory, while he was removed and taken to an officers' club to sing at a Christmas party. The Storm Troopers enjoyed his singing so much that they retained him as an entertainer to the end of the war. Eventually he reached Israel, where he recovered from his tragic loss, resumed his career as cantor, married again and fathered another family.

I have heard men and women curse God because of a business failure or stock market decline. This man, who had survived the most macabre kind of grief, stood on the pulpit each Shabbat to praise God in song. Could all of us have done this? Obviously, no. Don't ask me to believe, however, that free will is only an illusion when even a few can surmount the ultimate in crushing sorrow to affirm the potential dignity of human beings.

I have felt the irresistible pull of freedom in my own life. When I agonized over renouncing my pacifism, when I struggled between loving care for a sick wife and maintaining my own integrity, the forces on both sides were so evenly and painfully balanced that I felt like a rope in an emotional tug-of-war, pulled with such equal intensity from both sides that at any instant it would snap. Everything I had inherited or experienced, consciously or unconsciously, every factor in my environment, internal and external, entered into my decision. But in the last analysis it was I—my judgment, my conscience, my self—who had to decide. My freedom.

Will the world be any different—any better, any worse—for my having been here?

I hope so. I think so. One never really knows where a word, a gesture, a smile has profoundly affected other lives. An English professor of mine at Western Reserve University thought highly enough of a paper I had written to suggest my submitting it for publication. The only tangible consequence was my first collection of polite rejection slips. But my self-confidence and appetite for public print were boosted to the point where I can attribute a good part of my writing career to that simple act of encouragment.

I have already mentioned, in passing, my role in the lives of others. In my study at the Temple is a folder that I sometimes describe as my morale file. It contains letters of appreciation. The persons who wrote those letters have no way of knowing that when I feel resentful of ingratitude or downhearted in the face of failure, I turn for invigoration to that file. So I know that in both war and peace I have succeeded in leaving an impact on the lives of many individuals.

Like the young couple whose bright, beautiful, precocious little girl died before her fourth birthday. They relied on me to help them work through their grief, resolve their attitudes toward their two remaining children, decide in the course of time whether to conceive another child. Or the woman who approached me after I had lectured in Washington one night to tell me that she had come from a thoroughly assimilated Jewish family, didn't even consider herself to be in any meaningful way a Jew. She had, as she put it, been saved for Judaism by hearing me preach on radio, then reading one of my books. Or the Marine

211

private who wrote to me from a Navy hospital four months after D-day at Iwo:

> Dear Chaplain—
>   It all seems like a lifetime since our last meeting under very strenuous circumstances. As it comes back to me, the door of our Higgins Boat jammed as we hit the beach and we were ordered over the side. As I started up the beach the heavy equipment caused me to fall on my knees. As I was about to get up a very reassuring voice said, "Hello, Walter!" I'd like to say, sir, that those two words were about the most encouraging words I heard on that hell hole.

Fact is, I never saw this man on the beach. I distinctly recall saying good-bye to him on board ship just before he went over the side. His error of time and place, however, is nowhere near as important as the fact that simple words I had spoken remained in his tortured memory to give him strength.

Even more amazing is the letter I received from a total stranger who heard me speak at a service honoring the rabbi of his congregation. He came to that service agonizing over a man on his office staff who was suffering an intense emotional upheaval, hence no longer able to carry his share of responsibility effectively. My correspondent and his associates were torn between equally unhappy alternatives: whether to fire the man in question for the sake of business efficiency, or to jeopardize the success of their office by retaining him in the name of compassion.

The service at which I had spoken took place on Friday night. Tuesday's mail brought me a letter describing it as "a profoundly moving experience" and enclosing words the writer had dispatched that very day to his partners:

> On a business basis there would seem to be little reason to justify retaining Bob past the end of this month. Other

212

things keep coming to mind: a sick child, an anxious mother, a man struggling with overwhelming problems. . . .

Mary and I had supper and we spoke briefly about the matter but mostly I remained in a very thoughtful and troubled frame of mind. After supper we went to the Synagogue for Friday Evening Services. The occasion was a commemoration of Rabbi L.'s 40th anniversary in our congregation.

I came to the Synagogue out of respect and affection for a dear and good friend. I had no thought of looking for answers to the worldly problem which troubled me. It has never been my practice to seek help beyond the human resources available to me. . . .

Rabbi L. and Rabbi Gittelsohn both spoke of the need for a "place" where men could come together and seek communion with the spiritual forces of life and take strength from one another and that spiritual force of nature which pre-existed us on this planet.

If this is the stuff of which miracles are made, then maybe there was a small miracle last night, for I came away with the knowledge that it was not my strength alone which would have to cope with Bob's problems. There are other resources at hand and we must use them both for him and for ourselves, or there is indeed no meaning to human existence.

We must, in the days to come, convey to Bob and his family . . . that we will do our very best to lend him strength in a time of sore trial.

My sermon that night had been on theology, expressing ideas similar to those expounded in the last two chapters. I had not dealt with any personal dilemmas. I left the synagogue with the hope that I may have provided some modest food for thought, no more. Little did I dream that several human lives were so profoundly influenced by my words.

213

Let me not exaggerate. For most people, at most times, even the best of sermons provide little more than temporary diversion. Yet we who preach these sermons often underestimate their possible impact.

Yes, I rest satisfied that if there is a cosmic scale, it will reflect that the world may be a little better for my having been part of it. Not as much as I might have hoped, just a little; but enough to reassure me that I have not entirely wasted the life God gave me.

My days have been full. I have, thank God, found strength and help to survive the tribulations that have come to me as they do to everyone. No one of the battles I have fought is concluded yet; I shall continue to expend every ounce of my energy toward winning them. But what of my children? And their children and theirs? What does the future hold? "Watchman, what of the night?" And the morning?

One would have to be a moron to view today's world realistically without feeling deep fear. I said it earlier in commenting on my Iwo Jima sermon: "How easy it would be, in reading these words more than a generation after they were first spoken, to succumb to bleak despair. . . . I struggle intensely to escape the trap of pessimism toward which the facts of life often impel me." It would betray my temperament and disposition unconscionably for me even to give the appearance of being a Pollyanna. Yet I have not succumbed, and I shall continue to struggle with my final conscious breath. The dusk, which hangs so ominously overhead, may presage the death of human civilization. Or it may be the first, faint suspicion of light that heralds the rising sun.

Do I delude myself in clinging to hope? Sometimes it seems so. One seldom picks up a newspaper without reading of individuals and gangs who cheat and rob and kill at will. We too easily overlook the vast numbers of persons whose decency is never chronicled in the press or on newscasts. On a wintry day when the ground was covered with heavy snow, I had hospital visits to make in an urban ghetto neighborhood where many muggings had taken place. My car slid from the center of the street into a deep drift; the rear wheels spun futilely. Two men and four youngsters were clearing a nearby walk. When they saw my plight, without being asked, they came with their shovels to rescue me. One of them even drove my car to the next intersection where the main road had been cleared. The men refused any compensation but allowed the boys to accept the money I offered them for candy.

More recently, while driving up a remote road in southern New Hampshire to the top of a mountain, my car stalled. Two young men driving down the mountain stopped to ask if we needed help. One of them, a mechanic, was able to diagnose the trouble as a damaged battery that might explode. Though it meant getting dangerous acid on his hands, he stopped the leak, drove me five miles to the nearest service station for a new battery, returned me to my car, and waited to be sure the engine would start. He and his companion were enjoying a day off. Stopping to help me meant they would have to curtail their trip, but they stopped and helped. And tried to refuse the money I stubbornly thrust on them.

Neither rescue was reported in newscast or print. Every day, however, stories of violence and mayhem appear most prominently. We are constantly regaled also with accounts of businessmen and politicians whose conduct is inexcusably venal. So much so that we are apt to forget the millions who are honorable. We need to be reminded, lest all our hope be corroded. Such antidotes to debilitating pessimism can be found in each area of social concern where my career has been centerd.

The sphere of economics, for example. No one who is literate in economics and simultaneously cares deeply about human welfare can avoid being frightened by the cancerous growth of gargantuan international corporations that overshadow and dominate even the largest of governments. But there is reason to believe that more people are aware of this danger today than ever before. Ralph Nader has spurred the birth and growth of consumer interest groups as a third force in the traditional power struggle between the leaders of industry and labor. It is no longer considered rank heresy to urge that representatives of both consumers and workers be included on the boards of corporations. Industrialists and union leaders are coming closer to the common conclusion that neither can succeed in the long run without the other, that the best hope for both is an enlightened and socially responsible kind of capitalism.

By the spring of 1985, there were more than six thousand Employee Stock Ownership Plans (ESOP) involving over ten million employees in the United States.[1] They represented varying degrees of ownership and success; the important thing is that workers themselves are beginning to assume total or partial ownership of the firms for which they work. The political democracy which we hold so precious may yet be supplemented by a meaningful measure of democracy in the marketplace.

The outrageous stock-exchange scandals of 1986 and 1987 sent shudders of indignation and shame into the very substructure of American commerce. Yet they may yet prove to be the shock therapy that clears the way for a substantial cure. Without them, one wonders whether John Shad, Chairman of the Securities and Exchange Commission, would have contributed his gift of $20 million toward establishment of an extensive ethics program at the Harvard Graduate School of Business. If other business schools and groups can be encouraged to follow suit, the result could be a catharsis that cures.

Confronting massive immorality, we can give up in despair. We can surrender our society to imminent and ominous destruction. Or we can rebel with such vigor that we establish the turning point that can save us.

No less is true in Jewish life. Pessimists, alarmed by the increasing rates of mixed marriage and assimilation, have predicted the imminent disappearance of Judaism and Jews from the American scene. The dangers are real. But it is also real that the quality of Jewish education in the United States is improving dramatically; that involvement with Israel has infused new energy and vitality into the American Jewish community; that a larger proportion of Jews in this country than ever before is actively practicing Judaism rather than just passively professing Jewish faith.

The threat to Israel's survival is greater now than at any time since 1948. Yet even here there is reason for hope. The tactics and motives of Israel's Arab and Soviet enemies are becoming more transparent almost daily. The importance of Israel as a dependable ally against Russian expansionism is increasingly recognized even by some who bear no special love for Jews or a Jewish State. The new determination of Reform and Conservative Jews to open the vistas of religious pluralism adds strength to the probability that Israel will become what its founders intended, a state both Jewish and modern.

How about equal rights for minorities? Succumbing to discouragement is easy, resisting it difficult. But there are breaks in the clouds here too. An accurate comparison of conditions today with those during World War II discloses substantial progress—not enough by any means for

217

complacency but adequate at least for balance. In colleges, on faculties, in the professions, as executives, significantly larger numbers of Hispanics and Blacks are to be found now than in 1945.

Finally, the most portentous field of all—the threat of nuclear war, which could render this planet incapable of ever again sustaining life. Following the vagaries of the superpowers in their competition for arms and the frenetic drive of lesser powers to imitate them gives one the impression of madmen intent upon suicide. Yet even here I refuse to allow my fears to become self-fulfilling prophecies. Even here hope remains.

In the United States, new evidence accrues almost daily that masses of citizens are determined to play a role in the prevention of nuclear war. They are no longer willing to leave the decision of life or death up to so-called leaders who have repeatedly shown themselves to be blind. Labor unions—long among the advocates of massive armament as a means to higher industrial employment—are among the newest recruits to the peace forces. In February 1982 the Executive Council of the AFL-CIO for the first time questioned President Reagan's proposed increase in military spending. Since then more than twenty national labor unions have publicly called for a nuclear arms freeze.

In April 1987 tens of thousand of union members participated in a Mobilization for Justice and Peace, among them five of the country's six largest unions. Eight members of the AFL-CIO Executive Council were involved; several prominent union presidents were among the speakers.

Nearly a dozen state legislatures, hundreds of other legislative bodies, and an impressive number of Congressmen and Senators have supported the call for a nuclear freeze. In June of 1982, three-quarters of a million people jammed New York's Central Park and surrounding streets in what a park ranger described as "the world's largest peace rally ever."

At the same time, a high-level international commission chaired by former Prime Minister Olaf Palme of Sweden issued a report supporting substantial arms reduction by all nations for the sake of international security. Among the commission's seventeen members were high government officials, past and present, of this country, Russia, and Canada.

Equally impressive is the newly intensified interest of the group most qualified to urge nuclear restraint, the medical profession. Its voice is heard throughout the world, reminding us that survival of a nuclear war would be horrendous even if possible. The most hopeful aspect of the Budapest Conference toward this end, sponsored in June of 1985 by International Physicians for the Prevention of Nuclear War, is the fact that it was co-chaired by Dr. Bernard Lown of the United States and Dr. Eugeni Chazov, Deputy Minister of Public Health in the Soviet Union. The Conference called for a "complete moratorium on nuclear explosions by all nations on earth."

It would be inexcusably naive to pretend that the voice of the world's physicians is more yet than a warning whisper. But even a whisper can be heard; once recognized, moreover, it can stimulate louder voices.

New winds are stirring. New voices are sounding. The citizenry of all nations are commencing to heed these voices. They will no longer accept the passive helplessness of the past, the defeatist notion that they can do nothing to save themselves. New voices and new winds harbor hope for humanity.

These words are written with great anguish at a time when much of the world seems mired in a swamp of reaction. In politics, in economics, in international relations, in religion, too many of us yearn for childhood's simple, absolute certainties. Our quest could end in disaster. It could also prove to be but a temporary lapse in the pursuit of decency, justice, and peace. Armageddon remains possible. It is not inevitable.

Our Jewish tradition speaks of the *chevlay shel masheeach*, the excruciating turmoil and pain that must precede the coming of the messiah. Could our current anguish be that? Perhaps, but not just by wishing it so. Intentions and hopes—indispensable as they are—can be only beginnings; after adopting them, we need to act. A wonderful theme is etched on an interior wall of the Museum of the Diaspora in Tel-Aviv.

> To remember the past
> To live in the present
> To trust the future

Only if we remember the past accurately and live in the present fully can our trust in the future be redeemed.

One day, we are told, the disciples of Rabbi Nachum of Tshernibol sat reflecting on the significance of life. They decided that all would be meaningless were it not for their devoted teacher. So they arose and with united impulse set forth to join their rebbe. At that very moment, the rebbe himself, pondering the purpose and value of life, concluded that all would be waste were it not for the faithful few who followed him. So he arose too, walked to the door of his house, and saw his disciples coming to greet him. In that moment, it is said, "the circle was closed."

I live and pray and work for the time when the circle will be closed for all humankind, the circle of integrity within each person, the circle of love binding us to one another, the circle encompassing ourselves and God.

I remain harnessed to that hope.

Notes

1. *New York Times*, 20 April 1985.